A (VERY) SHORT INTRODUCTION TO BEGINNING POLISH GRAMMAR

A (very) Short Introduction to Beginning Polish Grammar

by
Jack J. Hutchens

MB
Modern Barbarian Press
Poznań, PL and Urbana, IL

A (very) Short Introduction to Beginning Polish Grammar
by Jack J. Hutchens © 2010

Published by Modern Barbarian Press, Poznań, Poland and Urbana, Illinois. All rights reserved. This book may not be reproduced in whole or in part, including illustrations, in any form (beyond that copyright permitted by Sections 107 and 108 of the U.S. Copyright Law and except by reviewers for the public press), without written permission from the publishers or author.
For information on other Modern Barbarian Press publications see the editor's page at http://www.lulu.com/spotlight/jackhutchens

ISBN 10 - 0-9791236-0-7
ISBN 13 - 978-0-9791236-0-3

About This Book

Polish is a West-Slavic language spoken by 40 million inhabitants of Poland, as well as millions of others around the world. With Poland's entrance into the European Union, knowledge of the Polish language has become important to international politics, business, and cultural studies.

The following work is not intended to be used alone as a comprehensive primer for Polish. It is an introductory reference grammar meant to be used in a Polish language course in conjunction with other workbooks that follow a more communicative approach to second language pedagogy. Some such books include Małgorzata Małolepsza's *Hurra Po Polsku!*, Aleksandra Janowska and Magdalena Pastuchowa's *Dzień Dobry*, and Professor Władysław *Miodunka's Cześć jak się masz?* The student of Polish should also invest in a good Polish-English dictionary that gives the conjugation patterns of verbs and declension patterns of nouns. Probably the best in this area is either the *Collins Praktyczny słownik Polsko-Angielski/Angielsko-Polski*, edited by Jacek Fisiak, or the *Berlitz Polish-English/English-Polish Dictionary*. Though the book attempts to put Polish grammar in an order according to its difficulty, the instructor should feel free to move around the book however best fits the class's needs.

The beginning student of Polish should use this book only as a tool in her/his study of Polish. It has been written with the beginning student in mind, purposely avoiding overly linguistic terminology, opting instead for simpler language in order to explain such complex ideas. (For a more in-depth, linguistic explanation, see Oscar Swan's *A Grammar of Contemporary Polish*, available for free in PDF on the Internet.) The grammatical elements of this book cover almost everything the beginning student is likely to encounter in the first two semesters of college level Polish language coursework. It is my hope that this grammar will help the beginning student make better (and easier) sense of the complexities of Polish grammar.

UWAGA!! Throughout the book you will come across sections beginning with "UWAGA!!" This literally means "attention." These sections will have something particularly important, to which you should pay special attention.

With all of this in mind I wish the student *powodzenia!*

•TABLE OF CONTENTS

1: The Polish Alphabet -- 2

2: Gender -- 3
- •Nouns -- 3
- •Adjectives -- 7

3: TheVerb -- 10
- •Tense and Verbal Aspect -- 11
- •Modal Verbs -- 15
- •Passive Voice --16
- •Imperative Mood -- 18

4: Case -- 23
- •Nominative -- 23
- •Accusative -- 25
- •Genitive -- 30
- •Instrumental -- 40
- •Locative -- 45
- •Dative -- 48
- •Vocative -- 53

5: Plurality -- 54
- •Numbers; Cardinal -- 54
- •Numbers; Ordinal -- 55
- •Nominative Plural -- 56
- •Accusative Plural -- 62
- •Genitive Plural -- 63
- •Instrumental Plural -- 66
- •Locative Plural -- 68
- •Dative Plural -- 69
- •Vocative Plural -- 69

6: Function Words -- 70

7: Time: Hours, Days, Months Years -- 72

–Appendix I: Declination Graphs -- 75

–Appendix II: Common Polish Verbs -- 77

–Appendix III: Verb Cards -- 79

–Appendix IV: Answers to Exercises -- 81

1: THE POLISH ALPHABET

The Polish alphabet is a bit longer than the English alphabet, having several letters that do not exist in English. Here is the alphabet in order:

A Ą B C Ć D E Ę F G H I J K L Ł M N Ń O Ó P R S Ś T U W Y Z Ź Ż

Luckily Polish pronunciation, though having some difficult consonant combinations, is extremely regular. It is important to consistently pronounce Polish vowels as they purely sound, meaning that one should never change the quality of a vowel. For example, in English the "uh" sound of "but" is quite often interchanged with other vowels. Polish vowels are always distinct and regular.

VOWELS:
a = father **e** = set **i** = "ee" in seed **o** = code

u = "oo" in boot **y** = "i" in bit

ą= nasal "o" as in French: "own" **ę**= nasal "e" as in French: "ewn"

DIPHTHONGS: A diphthong is the sound created by the combination of two vowels
ej = "a" in bate **aj** = "i" in bite **oj** = "oy" in boy

SPECIAL CONSONANTS: The following consonants have close English equivalents:
c = "ts"cats **ć** = "ch" in chop **j** = "y" yes **ł** (barred L) = "w" wind
ń = soft "n" **r** = a rolled "r" **ś** = "sh" in she **w** = "v" vine
ż = (zh) "s" in measure **ź** = similar to ż but softer

CONSONANT COMBINATIONS: As in English, Polish creates different consonants with the combination of two or more letters. The following English examples are only near equivalents:

ch = "h" in hot **sz & si** = "sh" in she **cz & ci** = "ch" in chop

rz = ż **dź / dzi** = "j" in jump **dż** = similar to "j" in jump but harder

2: GENDER

The first thing you have to understand about the Polish language is that, like most other European languages, it too has gender. All Polish nouns can be classified as **masculine**, **feminine**, or **neuter**. However, unlike languages such as French and German, the gender of nouns can usually be determined by way they end.

•NOUNS
•*MASCULINE* nouns most often end in a **consonant**:

stół – table	**dom** – home/house
długopis – pen	**lekarz** – doctor
ołówek – pencil	**nauczyciel** – teacher
pies – dog	**pisarz** – writer
profesor – professor	**komputer** – computer

•*Some masculine* nouns end in an "**a**":

kolega – colleague	**turysta** – tourist
poeta – poet	**mężczyzna** – man

•*FEMININE* nouns most often end with an "**a**":

książka – book	**koleżanka** – (female) colleague
tablica – blackboard	**kobieta** – woman
szkoła – school	**ulica** – street
matka – mother	**nauczycielka** – teacher

•*Some feminine* nouns end in a **consonant**:

rzecz – thing	**solidarność** – solidarity
wolność – freedom	**wilgoć** – humidity

UWAGA!! Most nouns that end in "**-ość**" are *feminine*, though one exception is "**gość**" – guest, which is *masculine*.

•*NEUTER* nouns usually end in an "**o**":

piwo – beer	**skrzydło** – wing
krzesło – chair	**pióro** – quill pen

•*Some neuter* nouns end in "**e**"   -**zebranie** – meeting
•*Some neuter* nouns end in "**ę**"   - **źrebię**– colt.
•*Some neuter* nouns end in "**um**" - **muzeum** – museum

•*Some Polish* nouns are always *plural*: **okulary**–glasses   **drzwi**-door/doors

•PRONOUNS

The following is the list of pronouns in Polish.

-Singular
ja - I
ty - you
on - he
ona - she
ono - it
pan - sir / Mr.
pani - mrs, ms., miss

-Plural
my - we
wy - you
oni - they (masc.)
one - they (non. masc.)
one
panowie - gentlemen / they (form.)
panie - ladies / they (form.)
państwo - ladies & gentlemen/Mr. & Mrs.

Since Polish nouns have gender, the pronouns that replace them also show gender. For example, though a "book" is an "it" in English, the Polish "*książka*" is an "*ona*," or "she" since it has feminine gender. Thus an "*ołówek*" [pencil] is an "*on*," or "he," and an "*okno*" [window] is an "*ono*," or "it."

As you will notice in the list above, modern Polish retains formal forms of "you." When speaking to a woman we do not know, or is in a higher position, or who is older, or to whom we wish to show some kind of formal respect we address her as "**Pani**." When speaking to a man on similar terms we use "**Pan**." Almost always the English translation is simply "you." "**Pan**" "**Pani**" can also be used to talk about a man or woman that we are not directly addressing. Look at the following examples:

Czy Pani jest zmęczona?   -Are you (speaking to a woman) tired?
Czy ta Pani jest zmęczona?   -Is that woman (over there) tired?

•REFLEXIVE PRONOUN: SIĘ

The reflixive pronoun *"się"* is a necessary part of some verbs, such as *"bać się"* "to be afraid." It also changes the meaning of some verbs, such as *"uczyć"* "to teach," versus *"uczyć się"* "to learn." Polish uses it for all persons. For example:

Boję się tego psa.   I'm afraid of that dog.
Boisz się tego psa.   You're afraid of that dog.
Boi się tego psa.   He/She is afraid of that dog.
Boimy się tego psa.   We're afraid of that dog.
Boicie się tego psa.   You all are afraid of that dog.
Boją się tego psa.   They are afraid of that dog.

As you can see, even though the subject of the sentence changes, the reflexive pronoun remains the same. This means that *"się"* can mean "myself," "yourself," "herself," etc. depending on the conjugation of the verb (see chapter 3 on verbs). For example:

Widzę się.	I see myself.
Widzisz się.	You see yourself.
Widzi się.	He/She sees him/herself.
Widzimy się.	We see ourselves/each other.
Widzicie się.	You all see each other.
Widzą się.	They see each other.

• **INTERROGATIVE PRONOUNS**

Interrogative pronouns (question words) act like adjectives, also having to agree with the nouns they qualify in gender.

• **KTÓRY, KTÓRA, KTÓRE**

"**Który**" is a question word that means "which" in English. It acts like an adjective and must agree in gender with the noun it qualifies.

-**Który** samochód jest nowy?	-Which car is new?
-**Która** jest godzina?	-What (Which) time (hour) is it?
-**Które** okno jest otware?	-Which window is open?
-**Które** okulary są moje?	-Which glasses are mine?

• **JAKI, JAKA, JAKIE**

"**Jaki**" is a question word that means "what kind of" in English. It also acts like an adjective and must agree in gender with the noun it qualifies.

-**Jaki** lubisz kolor?	-What [kind of] color do you like?
-**Jaka** jest pogoda dzisiaj?	-What is the weather like today?
-**Jakie** pijesz piwo?	-What kind of beer are you drinking?
-**Jakie** są te skrzypce?	-What kind of violin(s) is (are) that (those)?

• **CZYJ, CZYJA, CZYJE**

"**Czyj**" is a question word which translates as "whose" in English. Like other possessive pronouns it acts like an adjective, agreeing with the nouns in question according to gender and number.

-Czyj to ołówek?	-Whose pencil is that?
Czyj jest ten ołówek?	
-Czyja to książka?	-Whose book is that?
Czyja jest ta książka?	
-Czyje to krzesło?	-Whose chair is that?
Czyje jest to krzesło?	
-Czyje to pieniądze?	-Whose money is that?
Czyje są te pieniądze?	

UWAGA!! Note that "to be" ("*jest*" and "*są*") can be ommitted here, and that "***to***" still acts as a universal "that."

- **-Ś AFTER INTERROGATIVE PRONOUNS**

If we add *–ś* to the end of interrogative pronouns we get certain nouns. For example, "*kto*" means who, but "*ktoś*" means "someone" or "somebody." Look at the following examples:

Kto	– who?	**Ktoś**	– Somebody
Który	– which?	**Któryś**	– One
Co	– what?	**Coś**	– Something
Jaki	– what kind of?	**Jakiś**	– Some kind of

- **POSSESSIVE PRONOUNS**

In Polish, possessive pronouns act like adjectives, also having to agree with the nouns according to gender, number and case.

my	your (sing)	our	your (pl)
mój (masc)	**twój** (masc)	**nasz** (masc)	**wasz** (masc)
moja (fem)	**twoja** (fem)	**nasza** (fem)	**wasza** (fem)
moje (neut)	**twoje** (neut)	**nasze** (neut)	**wasze** (neut)

The following possessive pronouns never change for gender or number:

his	her	their
jego	**jej**	**ich**

Look at the following sentences and their use of possessive pronouns:

To jest twój ołówek.	-That is your pencil.
To jest moja książka.	-That is my book.
To jest nasze piwo.	-That is our beer.
To jest wasz dom.	-That is your (pl) home.
To jest jego matka.	-That is his mother.
To jest jej ojciec.	-That is her father.
To są ich pieniądze.	-That is their money.

UWAGA!! Notice the use of "**to**" in the previous sentences. Even though some of the nouns are masculine and feminine, "**to**" is still used. Here, instead of being used as "this," as in "**to piwo**" [this beer], it is functioning as a "pointing" word, demarcating a certain object.

- **SWÓJ, SWOJA, SWOJE**

The Polish possessive pronoun "**swój**" is extremely confusing, though it does eliminate certain ambiguities. Look at the following English sentence:

"He has his pencil."

Out of context the meaning of this sentence is ambiguous. Is it saying that "he" has "his own" pencil, or is it saying that "he" has a pencil that belongs to some other man? From the information given, we cannot determine this. Now look at the following two Polish sentences which, when translated, both mean the same thing as the English sentence:

(a) "**On ma jego ołówek.**"   (b) "**On ma swój ołówek.**"

Though these are both correct translations, there is none of the ambiguity found in the English sentence. Sentence (a) means: "He [**on**] has some other man's pencil." Sentence (b) means "He [**on**] has his *own* pencil." This is the confusion that is eliminated in Polish by the use of "**swój**" "**swoja**" "**swoje**".

Look at another example:

"She loves her father."

Again, in English, we have the same confusion as in the last example.

(a) "**Ona kocha swojego ojca.**"   (b) "**Ona kocha jej ojca.**"

Both sentences are correct translations of the English sentence. However, translation (a) means that a daughter loves her own father, whereas in translation (b) we have the beginnings of an intrigue, as "she" loves maybe her friend's father.

•ADJECTIVES

Not only do nouns have gender, but the adjectives that qualify (describe) them must agree with their gender as well. Again, this can be seen by the words' endings.

•*Masculine* adjectives end with "**y**" or "**i**". If an adjective ends in –k- or –g- then there will be an "-i" after it. For example:

dobry – good   **mały** – small
wysoki – tall   **drogi** – expensive/dear

•*Feminine* adjectives will end with an "**a**". For example:

dobra – good   **mała** – small
wysoka – tall   **droga** – expensive/dear

•*Neuter* adjectives, and *plural* adjectives will end with an "**e**". For example:

dobre - good   **małe** – small
wysokie – tall   **drogie** – expensinve/dear

UWAGA!! As you can see, the masculine adjective "*wysoki*" ends with "-*i*" and the neuter equivalent ends with "-*ie*." However, the feminine equivalent only ends with an "*a*." The reason for this is historical. Because of the way Polish has developed over the centuries there is never "-ke" "-ky" "-ge" or "-gy" at the end of a word. An "*i*" will always need to be placed after the "k" or "g" as we see above. There is no problem, however, with the "-ka" or "-ga" combinations.

•There are some adjectives that must end with "-i" in the masculine even though they do not end in "-k-" or "-g-":

tani – cheap   **głupi** – stupid   **średni** – medium

•To make these adjectives feminine we must leave the "-i" and add "a":
tania – cheap   **głupia** – stupid   **średnia** - medium

•To make these adjectives neuter we must leave the "-i" and add "e":
tanie – cheap   **głupie** – stupid   **średnie** – medium

•In Polish, most adjectives come before the nouns that they describe. For example:

M	F	N	Pl
-nowy ołówek	-nowa książka	-nowe krzesło	-nowe skrzypce
-dobry pisarz	-dobra szkoła	-dobre piwo	-dobre drzwi

• Tᴇɴ, Tᴀ, Tᴏ, Tᴇ
In Polish there are four words for "this/that" or "these/those." They act like adjectives and so must change according to the gender and number of the following noun:

Ten – masculine   **Ta** – feminine
To – neuter   **Te** – plural (these/those)

For example: -**Ten** długopis = This pen   -**Ta** książka = This book
              -**To** piwo = This beer   -**Te** drzwi = This (These) door(s)

If one wishes to differentiate between "this" thing and "that" thing over there, one can add "**tam**" [there] to "this." For example:

-**Tamten** długopis = That pen   -**Tamta** książka = That book
-**Tamto** piwo = That beer   -**Tamte** drzwi = That (Those) door(s)

Exercise 1: Match the adjectives from the first column with appropriate nouns in the second in the blanks below.

Adjectives:

~~dobry~~
mała
smaczne
stare
wysoka
mądra
biały
tani
czerwona
długa
drogie
duże
niski
przystojny

Nouns:

książka
okulary
długopis
drzwi
ołówek
kobieta
mężczyzna
dziecko
stół
~~pies~~
nauczycielka
piwo
farba
kawa

1. Ten _dobry pies_

2. Ta _____

3. To _____

4. Te _____

5. Ten _____

6. Ta _____

7. To _____

8. Te _____

9. Ten _____

10. Ta _____

11. Ten _____

12. Ta _____

13. Ten _____

14. Ta _____

3: THE VERB

As a highly **inflected** languge, Polish conjugates verbs according to each person in the present, past and future.

•BYĆ
The first Polish verb we need to learn is "*być*" which means "to be." You will find that nearly all Polish verbs end in "*ć*" and those that do not, will end in "*c*". Think of the final "*ć*" as the **to** of English infinitives.

Być
(ja) jestem　　　　(my) jesteśmy
(ty) jesteś　　　　(wy) jesteście
(on) jest　　　　　(oni) są
(ona) jest　　　　 (one) są
(ono) jest　　　　 (one) są
(pan) jest　　　　 (panowie) są
(pani) jest　　　　(panie) są
　　　　　　　　　(państwo) są

As you can see, "**być**" is not a very regular verb, much like "to be" in English. You will find that many Polish verbs are quite regular, however, following and fitting into certain patterns. We can divide Polish verbs into 5 categories according to their 1st person singular (*ja*) and 2nd person singular (*ty*) conjugations:

-am / -asz　　**-em / -esz**　　**-ę/ -isz**　　**-ę/ -ysz**　　**-ę/ -esz**

•COMMON POLISH VERBS
Here are some common Polish verbs that fit these patterns:

Mieć [to have]　　　　　　　　**Jeść** [to eat]
(ja) mam　　(my) mamy　　　　(ja) jem　　(my) jemy
(ty) masz　　(wy) macie　　　　(ty) jesz　　(wy) jecie
(ona) ma　　(oni) mają　　　　 (on) je　　　(one) jedzą

Czekać [to wait]　　　　　　　**Rozumieć** [to understand]
czekam　　czekamy　　　　　　rozumiem　　rozumiemy
czekasz　　czekacie　　　　　　 rozumiesz　　rozumiecie
czeka　　　czkają　　　　　　　rozumie　　　rozumieją

Lubić [to like]　　　　　　　　**Słyszeć** [to hear]
lubię　　　lubimy　　　　　　　słyszę　　　słyszymy
lubisz　　 lubicie　　　　　　　 słyszysz　　słyszycie
lubi　　　 lubią　　　　　　　　słyszy　　　słyszą

Czesać [to comb]		**Brać** [to take]	
czeszę	czeszemy	biorę	bierzemy
czeszesz	czeszecie	bierzesz	bierzecie
czesze	czeszą	bierze	biorą

As you have probably noticed, the pronoun is not necessary to know who is doing the action since the endings of each conjugation show all the information. For example, we know that "I" and not "you" is the subject of the sentence – "**Mam stół.**" [I have a table] – even though there is no "**ja**" before the verb, because the "**-am**" at the end provides this information.

•TENSE AND VERBAL ASPECT

Polish verbs have only three tenses; past, present, and future. However, they also have two aspects, **imperfective** and **perfective**. An example of an **imperfective** verb from the above list would be "*brać*." When this verb is conjugated we get the present tense:

•**Biorę lekarstwo.**   -I take medicine.

Out of context this could also be the present continuous tense:

•**Biorę lekarstwo.**   -I am taking medicine.

•SIMPLE FUTURE

The **perfective** verb paired with "*brać*" would be "*wziąć*." This also means "to take;" however, when we conjugate it we get the simple future tense:

•**Wezmę lekarstwo.**   -I will take medicine.

Most **imperfective/perfective** pairings are a bit easier to recognize as they often rely on prefixes:

Słuchać / Posluchać	to listen to
Czekać / Poczekać	to wait
Pisać / Napisać	to write
Jeść / Zjeść	to eat
Iść / Pójść	to go (by foot)

When the **perfective** is formed by simply adding a prefix, the conjugation patterns are similar:

ja słucham	ty słuchasz	ja posłucham	ty posłuchasz
ja czekam	ty czekasz	ja poczekam	ty poczekasz
ja piszę	ty piszesz	ja napiszę	ty napiszesz
ja jem	ty jesz	ja zjem	ty zjesz
ja idę	ty idziesz	ja pójdę	ty pójdziesz

Some **imperfective/perfective** pairings are a bit more complicated, involving a change in the middle:

- Dawać
- Dostawać
- Dać
- Dostać
- -to give
- -to get

Some **imperfective/perfective** pairings must simply be memorized as they look nothing alike:

- Brać
- Widzieć
- Mówić
- Wziąć
- Zobaczyć
- Powiedzieć
- -to take
- -to see
- -to speak, say, tell

As we see above, the **perfective** verb is used to relate the future. **Perfective verbs can never express the present**. Another difference between the **perfective** and **imperfective** that is important to keep in mind is that the **imperfective** expresses an **unfinished** action, and the **perfective** expresses a **finished** action. This is especially important to remember in the case of the past and imperfect future.

•THE PAST TENSE
Except for a few irregular verbs, the past tense is really quite easy to create in Polish. We begin with an infinitive, **być** (to be). We must first create what is called the **"L" form** of the verb.

-Step one:
  cut off the **ć** = **by_**
-Step two:
  add "**ł**" = **był** - "**L** form" of the verb for the singular masculine
-Step three:
  add the correct personal ending: **Ja** +**em**, **Ty** +**eś**, **On** + (**nothing**)

Byłem	– I was (man)
Byłeś	– You were (man)
Był	– He was, It (masc. noun) was

-To get the "**L** form" for singular feminine nouns you add an "**a**."

Byłam	– I was (woman)
Byłaś	– You were (woman)
Była	– She was, It (fem. noun) was

In the singular we also have a neuter form "**było**" –
Piwo było zimne   The beer was cold.

-To create the "L" form for **plural virile nouns** (meaning men only) change the "**ł**" to "**li**." We then add the appropriate personal ending to get the past:

My + **śmy**	= **Byliśmy**	– We were (men)
Wy + **ście**	= **Byliście**	– You were (men)
Oni + (nothing)	= **Byli**	– They were (men)

-To create the "L" form for plural feminine, non-virile masculine (not men), and neuter nouns add a "**y**," and then the appropriate personal ending for the past:

My + **śmy**	=**Byłyśmy**	– We were (all women)
Wy + **ście**	= **Byłyście**	– You were (all women)
One + (nothing)	= **Były**	–They were (women, animals, objects)

-In the past "**być**" is very regular. Some irregularities would include "**mieć**" (to have):

Ja – Miałem/Miałam   My – Mieliśmy/Miałyśmy
Ty – Miałeś/Miałaś   Wy – Mieliście/Miałyście
On – Miał   Oni – Mieli
Ona – Miała   One – Miały
Ono –Miało

Generally, verbs in the past are much more regular than verbs in the present, as in

"**czekać**" [to wait]
czekałem/am   czekaliśmy/łyśmy
czekałeś/aś   czekaliście/łyście
czekał/a/o   czekali/czekały

But then we have :

"**jeść**" [to eat]
jadłem/am   jedliśmy/łyśmy
jadłeś/aś   jedliście/łyście
jadł/a/o   jedli/jadły

• **IMPERFECTIVE FUTURE**
As stated above the simple future (perfective future) is created by conjugating the *perfective* verb. "**Zobaczę**" – "I will see." There also exists the future continuous (**imperfective future**). This is created with the appropriate future "**być**" form plus an *imperfective* verb in either the infinitive or L form.

Być (future)

będę	będziemy
będziesz	będziecie
będzie	będą

For example:

Będę czytać / Będę czytał/czytała.	-I will be reading.
Jak długo bedziesz czekać/czekał/czekała?	-How long will you be waiting?
Szymon bedzie jechać / jechał.	-Simon will be driving.

As you can see in the above examples, the *imperfective future* expresses actions in the future whose completion is not determined. **Though using the infinitive and the L form mean the same thing, Poles more commonly use the L form for this tense.**

If we look at the past and future imperfective and perfective forms side by side, the difference between the two becomes clearer:

•Imperfect past:
   Czytać:
Czytałem książkę gdy zadzwoniłeś.   -**I was reading** a book when you called.

•Perfect past:
   Przeczytać:
Przeczytałem tę książkę.   -I **read** that book / I **have read** that book.

In the first example the person did not finish reading the book. In the second example a male person read and finished reading the entire book. It could mean that he read it the night before, or that sometime in the past he "had" read it.

•Imperfect future:
   Czytać:
Będę czytał gdy przygotujesz się.   –I'll be reading while you get ready.

•Perfect future:
   Przeczytać:
Przeczytam ten artykuł w gazecie.   -I'll read this article in the newspaper.

In the first example there is no sense that the act of reading will be finished. It is something the person "will be doing" while something else happens. In the second example the person intends to read the entire article from start to finish. Though it may seem ambiguous, the sense of whether an act is completed or not is the major difference between the perfective and imperfective.

Look at two more examples:
Jechać:
Jechałem do Polski 10 razy.   -I have gone to Poland 10 times.

Pojechać:
Pojechałem do Polski latem.   - I went to Poland in the Summer.

We use the imperfective past in the first example to state something we have done a **number of times**. The perfective past in the second example states something we did **once**.

•MODAL VERBS

Polish modal verbs are quite functional and easy to use. They are as follows:

Chcieć [to want]		**Mieć** [supposed to]	
Chcę	Chcemy	Mam	Mamy
Chcesz	Chcecie	Masz	Macie
Chce	Chcą	Ma	Mają
L –	Chciał / Chcieli	L –	Miał / Mieli
	Chciała / Chciały		Miała / Miały

Móc [can, may]		**Umieć** [to know how to]	
Mogę	Możemy	Umiem	Umiemy
Możesz	Możecie	Umiesz	Umiecie
Może	Mogą	Umie	Umieją
L –	Mógł / Mogli	L –	Umiał / Umieli
	Mogła / Mogły		Umiała / Umiały

Musieć [must, have to]
Muszę   Musimy
Musisz   Muszicie
Musi   Muszą
L –   Musiał / Musieli
   Musiała / Musiały

***Powinien** [should]*

Powin**ienem/innam**   Powinn**iśmy/yśmy**
Powin**ieneś/innaś**   Powinn**iście/yście**
Powinien/Powinna   Powinni/Powinny

L – Powin**ienem/innam** był/a   Powinn**iśmy/yśmy** byli/były
   Powin**ieneś/innaś** był/a   Powinn**iście/yście** byli/były
   Powinien/Powinna był/a   Powinni/Powinny byli/były

To express any of the above simply conjugate the modal verb according to the person and tense (there are no perfective forms, so you would use the imperfective future for the future tense), plus an infinitive. For example:

Chcę oglądać film.	-I want to watch a movie.
Musisz poczekać na mnie.	-You have to wait for me.
Ma czytać tę książke.	-She's supposed to read that book.
Powinniśmy pojechać do domu.	-We should go home.
Możecie tu mieszkać.	-You all can live here.
Umieją gotować prowadzić.	-They know how to drive.

UWAGA!! Notice the difference between "**móc**" [can] and "**umieć**" [know how to]. **Móc** expresses what someone is allowed to do, while **umieć** expresses ability.

When negating "**musieć**" (**nie muszę**) remember that it means "don't have to." To express "musn't" you would negate "**móc**" (nie mogę).

•To express a modal verb in the future one MUST use the L form:

Będę chciał/a oglądać film.	-I will want to watch a film.
Będziesz musiał/a poczekać na mnie.	-You will have to wait for me.
Będziemy musieli/ały jechać do domu.	-We will have to go home.
Będziecie mogli/ły tu mieszkać.	-You all will be able to live here.
Będą umieli gotować prowadzić.	-They'll know how to drive.

•PASSIVE VOICE

The passive voice is used to form sentences where the subject is either unknown or is not as important as the action that is completed. In essence the object of the sentence takes on the qualities of the subject. For example:

ACTIVE: They make nice cars in Japan.
PASSIVE: Nice cars are made in Japan.

In this example, the subject of the active sentence is an unknown "they," so there is little difference when making it a passive sentence. It is still possible to make a sentence passive even if the subject is known. For example:

ACTIVE: Toyota makes nice cars.
PASSIVE: Nice cars are made by Toyota.

In a sense one could say that the subject of the passive sentence is still "Toyota;" however, grammatically the direct object "nice cars" has again taken on the role of the subject as in the first example.

The passive voice is not used nearly as often in Polish as it is in English. Unfortunately, the more formal version is rather difficult to create. However, there is a simpler version of the passive that is used in more colloquial, spoken Polish.

•CANONICAL PASSIVE

The more bookish form of the passive, or "canonical" passive, is made by connecting a conjugation of either *"zostać"* [to become] or *"być"* and then the passive participle of the main verb. For example:

Artykuł został napisany.	-The article was written.
Książka została przeczytana.	-The book was read.
Piwo zostało wypite	-The beer was drunk
Piwo zostanie wypite.	-The beer will be drunk.

With each of these examples we can include the subject as in the English example "by Toyota" with the preposition *"przez,"* "through." For example:

Artykuł został napisany przez Tomek. -The article was written by Tomek.

As you will notice in the above examples, the passive participle is an **adjective created from a verb**, which means that it will agree with the noun in gender, number and case just like any other adjective. Therefore, in the first sentence, the verb *"napisać"* becomes *"napisany"* in the participle, and since it qualifies the masculine noun *"artykuł"* it takes the *"y"* ending. Similarly, in the second sentence the verb *"przeczytać"* becomes *"przeczytana"* since it qualifies the feminine noun "*książka*," and in the third sentence, the verb *"wypić"* becomes *"wypite"* as it qualifies the neuter noun "*piwo.*" As you can see by the "-*any*" "*ana*" and "-*ite*" endings, there are different ways of creating the participle, depending on the verb.

malować	-to paint	malowany	-painted
pić	-to drink	pity	-drunk
myć	-to wash	myty	-washed
szyć	-to sew	szyty	-sewn
otworzyć	-to open	otwarty	-openend
tworzyć	-to create	tworzony	-created
palić	-to smoke	palony	-smoked
mleć	-to mill	mielony	-milled

As these examples illustrate, there is no one uniform way to create the participle. While studying the verbs you will want to include the participles in your notes to help in memorizing them.

•IMPERSONAL PASSIVE

The more colloquial or "impersonal" passive is easier to create and is used much more often in spoken Polish. It is created with a third person singular or plural conjugation of the verb with the reflexive prounoun *"się."*

Pije się dużo wódki w Polsce.	-A lot of vodka is drunk in Poland.
Pisało się kilka książek.	-A few books were written.
Piecze się chleb.	-The bread is baking.
Film już się zaczął.	-The film has already started.
Pisało się w gazecie.	-It was written in the newspaper.

This colloquial version of the passive is used for much the same reason as the more bookish version; that is, if the subject is unknown or is not as important as the rest of the information in the sentence.

•IMPERATIVE MOOD

The imperative form of the verb is used to make commands when using the second person singular or plural, and suggestions when using the first person plural. The formation of the imperative is relatively regular and depends on how the verb originally conjugates.

• Ę / ESZ, Ę / YSZ, Ę / ISZ VERBS

Verbs that conjugate in the first and second person singular as "ę/esz," "ę/ysz," or "ę/isz" form the imperative by dropping the last vowel or vowels of the **third person singular** conjugation. Sometimes this demands a slight spelling change, as you will see with *"bać się."* For example:

pisać	- pisze	= Pisz!	Write!
pić	- pije	= Pij!	Drink!
malować	- maluje	= Maluj!	Paint!
pluć	- pluje	= Pluj!	Spit!
robić	- robi	= Rób!	Do!
słyszeć	- słyszy	= Słysz!	Hear!
bać się	- boi się	= Bój się	Be afraid!

• AM / ASZ & EM / ESZ VERBS

Verbs that conjugate in the first and second person singular as "am/asz" or "em/esz" form the imperative by dropping the *"ą"* from the **third person plural** conjugation. For example:

czekać	- czekają	= Czekaj!	Wait!
czytać	- czytają	= Czytaj!	Read!
słuchać	- słuchają	= Słuchaj!	Listen!
powiedzieć	- powiedzą	= Powiedz!	Tell!
rozumieć	- rozumieją	= Rozumiej!	Understand!

- **USES OF THE IMPERATIVE**

When using any of these examples of the imperative, you would be speaking to one person.

Czekaj na mnie!	- Wait for me.
Pisz swój esej!	- Write your essay.
Nie bój się psa!	- Don't be afraid of the dog.

When addressing more than one person, you would need to add the third person plural ending *"-cie."*

Czekajcie na mnie!	- (You all) Wait for me.
Piszcie swoje eseje!	- (You all) Write your essays.
Nie bójcie się psa!	- (You all) Don't be afraid of the dog.

We can also use the imperative with the **first person plural** ending *"-my"* to mean "Let's" do something.

Czekajmy na niego.	- Let's wait for him.
Piszmy swoje eseje.	- Let's write our essays.
Nie bójmy się psa.	- Let's not be afraid of the dog.

- **THE CONDITIONAL**

Conditional sentences expressing possibility are structured slightly differently than in English. Look at the following examples:

Jeśli go zobaczę, powiem mu o tym.
-If I see him, I'll tell him about it.

Gdy pojadę do Chicago, odwiedzę rodzinę.
-When I go to Chicago, I'll visit my family.

Jeśli będzie miała czas, pójdzie na koncert.
-If she has time, she'll go to the concert.

As you can see in the above examples, Polish uses the future tense in both clauses of the conditional. The first example literally says "If I **will** see him, I'll tell him." The second example literally says "When I **will** go to Chicago, I'll go to Wrigley Field." In English, the first clause uses the present tense, while only the second clause uses the future. This must be kept in mind when creating conditional sentences. This is also the case when asking questions in the conditional. For example:

Co zrobisz, kiedy pojedziesz do Chicago?
-What will you do, when you (will) go to Chicago?
Jesli go zobaczysz, czy powiesz mu o tym?
-If you (will) see him, will you tell him about it?

•The Subjunctive

The subjunctive expresses unreal situations, dreams, and wishes. In order to construct the subjunctive we must use the word "gdyby," "if would" and the L form of the verb. For example:

Gdybym był prezydentem, miałbym dobre życie.
-If I were president, I'd have a good life.

Gdybyś miał czas, mógłbyś pójść ze mną.
-If you had time, you could come with me.

The endings one must remember for the subjunctive are:
ja – bym   my – byśmy
ty – byś   wy – byście
on – by   oni – by
ona – by   one – by

Literally, "gdybym" means "if I would," "gdybyś" "if you would," "gdyby" "if she/he would," etc. After this phrase we then have to add the L form of the verb which corresponds to the gender of the subject.

Gdybym miał – If I had (masc.)
Gdybym miała – If I had (fem.)

Gdybyś miał – If you had (masc.)
Gdybyś miała – If you had (fem.)

Gdyby miał – If he had
Gdyby miała – If she had

This is the same for plural subjects.

Gdybyśmy mieli – If we had (vir.)
Gdybyśmy miały – If we had (non vir.)

Gdybyście mieli –If you all had (vir.)
Gdybyście miały – If you had (nonvir.)

Gdyby mieli – If they had (vir.)
Gdyby miały – If they had (non. vir.)

To construct the second clause we must put the L form of the verb in front of the personal endings. For example:

...miałbym czas –I'd have time (masc.)
..miałabym czas –I'd have time (fem.)

...miałbyś czas – you'd have time (masc.)
...miałabyś czas – you'd have time (fem)

...miałby czas – he'd have time
...miałaby czas – she'd have time

Plural:

...mielibyśmy czas – we'd have time (vir.)
...miałybyśmy czas – we'd have time (non vir)

...mielibyście czas – you'd all have time (vir)
...miałybyście czas – you'd all have time (non vir)

...mieliby czas – they'd all have time (vir)
...miałyby czas – they'd all have time (non vir)

Exercise 2: Change the following verbs into the conditional form, for both genders where appropriate, according the the person in ( ). For example:

*iść (ty) _szedłbym / szłabym_

1: dać (ja) _____

2: być (ty) _____

3: zobaczyć (on) _____

4: kochać (my) _____

5: przeczytać (oni) _____

6: myśleć (one) _____

7: kupić (ona) _____

Exercise 3: Create conditional sentences according to the following example:
*gdyby (ty-masc.) potrzebować tego / (ja-fem) dać ci to:

Gdybyś potrzebował tego, dałabym ci to.

1: gdyby (on) przeczytać gazetę / (on) wiedzieć o tym

2: gdyby (oni) mieć pieniądze / (oni) móc to kupić

3: gydby (ty-fem) kochać mnie / (ja-masc) móc spać

4: gdyby (ja-fem.) być bogata / (ja-fem) mieszkać w pałacu

4: CASE – NOUNS & ADJECTIVES

Probably the most confusing and difficult, but also the most important thing to grasp about Polish is *case*. Case is the way nouns and adjectives change (*decline*) according to what function they serve in a sentence. Often these word changes (*declinations*) are used instead of prepositions, like "to" and "for." In Polish there are 7 cases. In a way, English also has cases.

•NOMINATIVE; KTO? CO? KTOŚ, COŚ

Like Polish, English has the *Nominative* (***Mianownik***) or "subject" case. This case denotes the subject of a sentence. For example:

    •(Ja) Jestem stary.   -I am old.

In this sentence the "**Ja**," "I" is the subject of the sentence, since it is the one performing the action of "being."

    •Pies jest młody.   -The dog is young.

Here "**pies**," "the dog" is the subject since it is the one performing the action. Look at the following examples:

    •Ten stary facet lubi śpiewać.   -That old guy likes to sing.

Here "**ten stary facet**" is the subject as he is the one 'liking' to sing.

    •Młody pies dużo je.   -The young dog eats a lot.

Here the "**młody pies**" is the one performing the action of eating "**je**," and so it is the subject.

•PERSONAL PRONOUNS

We have already seen the personal pronouns in the nominative case in the discussion of the verb:

Ja – I	My – we
Ty – you	Wy – you (pl)
Ona – she	One – they (fem)
On – he	Oni – they (masc)
Pani – you/she (formal)	Panie – you/they (frml pl / the ladies)
Pan – you/he (formal)	Panowie – you/they (frml pl/ gentlemen)
	Państwo - ladies and gentlemen

- **Questions** in the nominative case would be formed as in the following examples:

Kto to jest?	-Who is that?
Kto ma pieniądze?	-Who has money?
Co to jest?	-What is that?
Co to jest za budynek?	-What building is that?
Jaki jest twój brat?	-What is your brother like?
Jaka była ta kawa?	-What kind of coffee was that?
Który samochód jest lepszy?	-Which car is better?
Która książka jest ciekawa?	-Which book is interesting?
Czyj to jest dom?	-Whose house is that?
Czyja to jest woda?	-Whose water is that?

Exercise 4: Complete the following sentences by filling in the blanks with the correct form of "this" or "these" and the correct gender of the adjective in ( ). **Look up any words that you do not understand.**

1: ___ ołówek jest _____ (nowy).
   Ten ołówek jest nowy.

2: ___ książka jest _____ (drogi).

3: ___ piwo jest _____ (zimny).

4: ___ okulary są _____ (stary).

5: ___ dziecko jest _____ (młody).

6: ___ drzwi są _____ (duży).

7: ___ szklanka jest _____ (mały).

8: ___ dom jest _____ (zielony).

9: ___ nauczycielka jest _____ (mądry).

10: ___ mężczyzna jest _____ (wysoki).

•ACCUSATIVE; KOGO? CO? KOGOŚ, COŚ

English also has an equivalent to the *Accusative* (**Biernik**) case, which is called the direct object, or the receiver of the action of the subject in a sentence. For example:

-I have a pencil.

Here the "I" is the subject, as it is doing the "having," and the "pencil" is the direct object, as it is being "had" by the subject. In Polish the sentence would be:

-(Ja) Mam ołówek.

•MASCULINE NOUNS
"**Ja**" is the doer, and "**ołówek**" is the thing receiving the doing in the previous sentence. Here, because **ołówek** is an *inanimate masculine* noun **it does not change**. But now look at the following sentence:

(Ty) Masz kota.   -You have a cat.

Originally, cat is "**kot**." But because it is an *animate (living) masculine* noun an "-**a**" must be added to the end to fit it into the *accusative* case.

As discussed in the section on gender, some masculine nouns end in "-**a**".

Widzę mężczyznę.   -I see a man.
Znam poetę   -I know a poet

Though "*mężczyzna*" is an *animate masculine noun*, it ends with an "-**a**," and so declines similarly to feminine nouns by changing the "-**a**" to "-**ę**."

•FEMININE NOUNS
Look at the following sentence.

(On) Ma książkę.   -He has a book.

Originally, book is "*książka*," But because it is a *feminine* noun the ending "-**a**" must be changed to an "-**ę**" to fit it into the *accusative* case.

Feminine nouns end in a consonant do not change in the accusative.

Czytam powieść.   -I am reading a novel.

Though "*powieść*" is a *feminine* noun, it ends with a consonant, and so acts similarly to *inanimate masculine nouns* and does not decline in the *accusative*.

•Neuter Nouns
Neuter nouns, *like inanimate masculine* nouns do not change in the *accusative*.

Czy Pan ma piwo?   -Do you (sir) have beer?

Therefore, even though "*piwo*" is the *direct object* it looks the same in the *nominative* as it does in the *accusative*. This is true for all neuter nouns no matter what ending they have.

UWAGA!! The *accusative* case must be used with **transitive** verbs, that is, verbs that always have a *direct object*. For example; to have, to see, to like, to love, etc. You will **never** have the *accusative* case after **intransitive** verbs. For example; to be, to go, to become, etc. The *nominative* case (subject) will be used with these verbs.

•Adjectives and Possessive Pronouns
As mentioned above, adjectives and possessive pronouns must not only agree with their nouns according to their gender but also according to their case. We have already seen how adjectives appear in the *nominative* case:

Ten pies jest dobry.	-This dog is good.
Ta książka jest długa.	-This book is long.
Czy to jest dobre piwo?	-Is that good beer?
Te drzwi są duże.	-This door is big.

In the *accusative* case adjectives must decline according to the nouns they describe.

Mam *dobrego psa*.	-I have a good dog.
Oni mają *nowy dom*.	-They have a new home.
Czytasz *długą książkę*.	-You are reading a long book.
Czytam *twoją powieść*.	-I am reading your novel.
Ten bar ma *dobre piwo*.	-That bar has good beer.

UWAGA!! As you will notice, just as *inanimate masculine* nouns do not change in the *accusative* their adjectives **also do not change**. However, even though *feminine* nouns that end with a consonant do not change, **their adjectives will**.

•Ten Ta To Te
"Ten" "ta" and "to" also act similarly to adjectives. Look at the following examples of these words in the *accusative*:

Widzę *ten* dobry ołówek.	-I see that good pencil.
Czytam *tę* dobrą książkę.	-I'm reading this good book.
Czy pijesz *to* dobre piwo?	-Are you drinking that good beer.
On lubi *tego* dobrego psa.	-He likes that good dog.

•Personal Pronouns

We have already seen the personal pronouns in the nominative case. If a pronoun is the direct object of a sentence it, like other nouns, must decline. This is a point of similarity between English and Polish. One would not say in English "I know she," or "She loves he." These sentences would have to be "I know her," and "She loves him." The following graph shows pronouns in the accusative case next to their nominative originals:

Nom	Acc
ja	mnie
ty	cię/ (na) ciebie
on	go / (na) niego
ona	ją / (na) nią
ono	je / (na) nie
pan	pana
pani	panią
my	nas
wy	was
oni	ich / (na) nich
one	je / (na) nie

Look at the following examples:

Czy lubisz mnie?	–'**ja**,' 'I' becomes '**mnie**,' 'me.'
Znam cię!	–'**ty**,' 'you' becomes '**cię**,' 'you.'
Ona go kocha.	–'**on**,' 'he' becomes '**go**,' 'him.'
On ją kocha.	–'**ona**,' 'she' becomes '**ją**,' 'her.'
Czy oni nas znają?	–'**my**' 'we' becomes '**nas**' 'us'
Czy ona was znają?	–'**wy**,' 'you' (pl) becomes '**was**,' 'you' (pl).
Widzę ich.	–'**oni**,' 'they' becomes '**ich**,' (pl. masc.)
Czy widzisz je?	–'**one**' 'they' (pl. f. & n.) becomes '**je**,' (pl. f. & n.)

Czytam gazetę.	–gazeta –feminine noun, 'ona.'
= Czytam **ją**.	
Znam tego psa.	–pies –masculine noun, 'on.'
= Znam **go**.	
Widzę to okno.	–okno –neuter noun, 'ono.'
= Widzę **je**.	

You'll notice that some pronouns have longer versions. These are the forms that must be used after prepositions; for example after "*czekać na...*" "to wait for."

Czekam na **ciebie**.	-I'm waiting for you.
Czekam na **niego**.	-I'm waiting for him.
Czekam na **nią**.	-I'm waitng for her.
Czekam na **nie**.	-I'm waiting for it/them.
Czekam na **nich**.	-I'm waiting for them.

•ACCUSATIVE AFTER PREPOSITIONS

In some circumstances, the accusative is used after certain prepositions. This is especially true in the case of verbs of motion. For example:

Idę na koncert. —I'm going to the concert.

In Polish, one does not go "to" a concert, but "onto" a concert.

The same is true about going "onto" meetings. One also goes "onto," and not "to" the post office, "na **pocztę**," and a city sqaure, "na **rynek**."

Idzie na zebranie. —She's going to the meeting.

If someone is "at" a concert we would use the *locative* case (see page 42):

Jesteśmy na koncer**cie**. —We're at the concert.

If someone is going "to" the concert we use the *accusative*:

Jedziemy na koncer**t**. —We're driving to the concert.

Look at the following examples:

Długopis leży na sto**le**. —The pen is lying on the table.
Odkładam długopis na stół. —I'm putting the pen on(to) the table.

In the first example we must use the *locative*, because the pen "is located" on the table. In the second example we must use the *accusative* as we are placing the pen "onto" the table; **it is in motion**.

The preposition "**w**" means "in" when used with the *locative*.

Wino jest w butel**ce**. —The wine is in the bottle.

When used with the *accusative*, "**w**" means "into."

Nalewam wino w butel**kę**. —I'm pouring the wine in(to) the bottle.

We also use "w" and the *accusative* to tell what sport we're playing:

Gram w piłkę nożą. — I play soccer (foot ball).
Gra w koszykówkę. — He's playing basketball.

• **Questions** in the *accusative* are formed according to the following examples:

Kogo widzisz?	-Whom do you see?
Kogo znasz?	-Who do you know?
Co chcecie?	-What do you all want?
Co oglądasz?	-What are you watching?
Jaki masz ołówek?	-What kind of pencil do you have?
Którą czytasz książkę?	-Which book are you reading?
Czyjego psa widzisz?	-Whose dog do you see?
Jakie lubisz piwo?	-What kind of beer do you like?

Exercise 5: Fill in the blanks with the correct form of the verb "**mieć**" and the correct accusative form of the nouns in ( ). Look up any new vocabulary.
1: (Ja) _____ (pies) - <u>Mam   psa</u>•.
(Sometimes, when a noun changes according to case, vowels in the middle of the word will drop out. These are called "*fleeting vowels*.")

2: (My) _____ (lampa).

3: Ta pani _____ (torba).

4: Andrzej _____ (portfel).

5: Ten rolnik _____ (koń).

6: (Oni) _____ (telewizor).

Exercise 6: Fill in the blanks with the correct case forms of the adjectives and nouns in ( ).

1: Dawid i Halina mają_____ (biały pies).

2: Michał zna _____ (moja siostra).

3: Ania czyta _____ (długa książka).

4: Zosia czeka na _____ (jego brat).

5: Czy ona kupi _____ (nowa sukienka)?

6: Grzegorz prowadzi _____ (niebieski samochód).

7: Wasz dom ma _____ (duże okno).

•GENITIVE; KOGO? CZEGO? KOGOŚ, CZEGOŚ

The **Genitive** (*Dopełniacz*) case can also be seen in English. Its main function is to show possession. For example:

"The cat's ball...."

Originally, the English word is "cat;" however to show that it is the possessor of the ball an -**'s**- is added to the end of the word. In Polish this phrase would be:

"Piłka kota...."

As noted above, "*kot*" is the Polish for cat. By adding an "*a*" to end of the word we basically do the same thing as adding an -**'s**- to "cat." Notice that in Polish the possesser (most often) comes after the object being possessed. It is helpful, therefore to think of the genitive as "**of**" rather than -**'s**-. So the phrase would rather be read as "The ball of the cat..." You may notice that the genitive works similarly to the "de" of French or Spanish, and the "von" of German.

•MASCULINE NOUNS

As you have already learned, "*kot*" is a *masculine* noun, and so to make it *genitive* an "*a*" is added to the end. This is the case for all **animate masculine** nouns that end in a consonant.

Dom brata...	-Home of (my) brother...
Jedzenie psa...	-The food of the dog....
Kot Adama...	-The cat of Adam...
Ogród sąsiada..	-Garden of (my) neighbor...
Samochód ojca...	-The car of (my) father...
Biurko profesora..	-The professor's desk...

For **inanimate masculine** nouns an "*a*" is sometimes added to the end, but a "*u*" is also sometimes added. For English speakers the reasons may seem arbitrary, but there is somewhat of a system. **Inanimate masculine** nouns that are *small* quite often change into "*a*."

Łańcuszek klucza...	-Chain of the key/Keychain...
Typ ołówka...	-The type of pencil...
Koszt kolczyka...	-The cost of the earing...
Długość widelca...	-The length of the fork...

An unfortunate common exception to this is "*długopis*" "pen," which declines in the genitive as "długopis*u*."

Larger inanimate masculine nouns and masses often change into "*u*."

Silnik samochodu...	-The engine of the car...
Smak ryżu...	-The taste of rice...
Drzwi domu...	-The house's door...
Kilo cukru...	-A kilogram of sugar...

Borrowed words tend to take the "*a*" ending.

Ekran komputera...	-The screen of the computer..
Gracz tenisa...	-A player of tenis...

These are of course general rules. In the beginning you'll quite often need to look up the nouns to make sure of their declination.

Masculine nouns that end in "*a*" decline like feminine nouns, taking the "*y*" ending in the *genitive*.

Samochód mężczyzny...	-The man's car...
Wiersz poety...	-The poet's poem

- **FEMININE NOUNS**

Feminine nouns are much more regular than masculine nouns. Feminine nouns will end either in a "*y*" or in an "*i*" depending on the last consonant of the word.

Pies Anny...	- Anna's dog...
Smak kawy...	-The taste of coffee...
Dzień pracy...	-A day of work...
Dom babci...	-Grandma's house...
Siła nogi...	-The strength of the leg...
Kelner restauracji...	-A waiter of the restaurant...
Obywatel Anglii...	-A citizen of England...

UWAGA!! When feminine nouns end in "*ia*" as in "*babcia*" the *genitive* will simply drop the "*a*" giving us "*babci*," "grandma's." The exception to this would be in **borrowed** words and words for countries, which change the final "*a*" to an "*i*" as in "*Anglia*," which becomes "*Anglii*," "*England's*."

Feminine nouns that end in a **consonant** will also end in "*y*" or "*i*" depending on the preceding consonant.

Ciemność nocy...	-The dark of night...
Trudność gramatyki...	-The difficulty of grammar...

• Neuter Nouns

Neuter nouns are also more regular than masculine nouns and will always end in an "*a*."

Marka piwa...	-The brand of beer...
Wzrost drzewa...	-The height of the tree...
Burmistrz miasta...	-The mayor of the city...
Naczelnik więzienia...	-The prison's warden...
Właściciel źrebia...	-The owner of the colt...

Neuter nouns that end in "*-um*" are usually words borrowed from Latin. They do not decline in the singular.
Pracownik muzeum...   -A worker of the museum...
Sklepy centrum...   -Stores of the centre (downtown)...

UWAGA!! Notice that the "*o*" in "*piwo*," "*drzewo*," and "*miasto*" all become "*a*," the "*e*" of "*więzienie*" becomes "*a*," and the "*ę*" of "*źrebię*" becomes "*a*." Except for the "*um*" ending of "*muzeum*" and "*centrum*" the neuter will end in "*a*" in the genitive.

• The "Negative Direct Object"

Aside from showing possession, there are a few other reasons the genitive is used. The first is the **"negative" direct object**. You have already seen what the direct object is in the discussion of the *accusative* case. When the direct object is in a *negative* sentence, the noun takes on the *genitive* and not the accusative case.

• Masculine Nouns

(Ja) Mam ołówek.	-I have a pencil.	-positive sentence
(Ja) Nie mam ołówk*a*.	-I don't have a pencil.	-negative sentence
Prowadzę samochód	-I drive a car.	-positive
Nie prowadzę samochod*u*.	-I don't drive a car.	-negative

This, of course, is quite simple with direct objects that are *animate masculine* nouns since the accusative form is already similar to the genitive:

(On) Ma kota.	-He has a cat.
Nie ma kot*a*.	-He doesn't have a cat.

• Feminine nouns

(Ona) Pije kawę.	-She drinks coffee.
Nie pije kaw*y*.	-She doesn't drink coffee.
Czytają gazetę.	-They read the paper.
Nie czytają gazet*y*.	-They don't read the paper.

- **NEUTER NOUNS**

Jan pije piwo	-Jan is drinking a beer.
Jan nie pije piw*a*.	-Jan is not drinking a beer.
Ewa lubi muzeum.	-Ewa likes the museum.
Ewa nie lubi muze*um*.	-Ewa doesn't like the museum.

- **"Nie ma"**

A very important use of the **negative direct object** is the idiomatic expression *"nie ma,"* "there is none," or "is not here." For example, if asked: "Is there any coffee" *"Czy jest kawa?"* the negative answer would have to be: *"Nie ma kawy."* This expression is also used to say that someone isn't at home:

(on the phone)
Czy jest Michał w domu?	-Is Michał at home?
Nie, nie ma Michała.	-No, Michał's not home.
Nie, nie ma *go* w domu.	-No, he's not home

(in a restaurant)
Czy jest cukier?	-Is there any sugar?
Nie, nie ma cukr*u*.	-No, there isn't any sugar.

Though this idiom uses the **3rd person singular**, it would remain the same in reference to plural subjects. For example:

Czy *są* Marta i Ewa w pracy?	-Are Marta and Ewa at work?
Nie, nie *ma* Mart*y* ani Ew*y* w pracy.	-Marta and Ewa are not at work.
Nie, nie *ma ich* w pracy.	-No, they're not at work

This use of the *genitive* remains the model for talking about the future. However, instead of "*ma*" one would use the future of "to be," "*będzie*" for every person. For example:

Czy będzie kawa?	-Will there be any coffee?
Nie, nie będzie kawy.	-No, there will not be any coffee.

As with "*nie ma*" the use of the **3rd person singular** also works with plural subjects in the future. For example:

Czy *będą* Marek i Ewa?	-Will Marek and Ewa be here?
Nie, nie *będzie* ich.	-No, they will not be here.

- **CERTAIN VERBS**

Another reason the *genitive* is used is really quite arbitrary. It is simply used for the direct object after **specific verbs**. Here are a few examples:

Szukać – to look for:
Szukamy ksiazki — -We're looking for a book.

Używać – to use:
Używam ołówka. — -I'm using a pencil.

Słuchać – to listen to:
(Oni) Słuchają muzyki. — -They're listening to music.

Uczyć się – to learn:
(Ona) Uczy się języka. — -She's learing a language.

Uczyć – to teach:
(Ja) Uczę matematyki. — -I teach math.

Potrzebować – to need:
(Ty) Potrzebujesz przerwy! — -You need a break!

Bać się – to be afraid of:
Pies boi się kota. — -The dog is afraid of the cat.

Życzyć – to wish (someone sth)
Życzę szczęśćliwego Nowego Roku! — -Happy New Year!

These are only a few of many other examples of verbs that demand the genitive for a direct object.

•AFTER CERTAIN PREPOSITIONS
The genitive case is also used after certain prepositions:

Do – to
(Oni) Jadą do Polski. — -They're going to Poland.
(Ja) Idę do domu. — -I'm going home.

Z – from
(Ona) Jest z Kanady. — -She is from Canada.
To jest pociąg z Krakowa. — -That's the train from Cracow.

Od – from
Mam to od Marka. — -I have this from Marek.
Będę tam od marca. — -I'll be there from March.
Jak daleko jest od Berlina do Pragi. — -How far is it from Berlin to Prague?

U – at
Mieszkam u Jana. — -I'm living at Jan's place.
Byłem u siostry. — -I was at my sister's.

Dla – for
To jest dla *ciebie*.   -This is for you.
To jest wielki szok dla *niego*.   -That's a great shock for him.

Oprócz – except for
Oprócz *tego*, to jest dobry pomysł.   -Except for that, it's a good idea.

Zamiast – instead of:
(On) Chce wodę, zamiast *koli*.   -He wants water instead of a soda.

Wśród – among:
Są zdrajcy wśród nas!   -There are traitors among us!

Obok – next to
    obok poczt*y*   -next to the post office

UWAGA!! Notice above that the two words for "from" are "*z*" and "*od*." The preposition "*z*" will never be used in reference to a person since it literally has the meaning "**from out of**." It will only be used in reference to cities, places, countries, containers, etc. "*Od*" is used in time expressions – "*od pierwszej do drugiej*" [from one to two] – in expressing the idea of getting something from someone – "*Mam to od Ewy*" [I have this from Ewa] – or to express the distance between to points, for example two cities – "*od Berlina do Warszawa*" [from Berlin to Warsaw].

- **AMOUNTS**

The genitive is also used after denominators of amounts:

Dużo – much, many, a lot of
    dużo czas*u*   -a lot of time
    dużo wod*y*   -a lot of water

Mało – little, not much
    mało chleb*a*   -little bread
    mało czas*u*   -not much time

Więcej – more
    więcej światł*a* -more light
    więcej win*a*   -more wine

Mniej – less, fewer
    mniej wódk*i*   -less vodka
    mniej smak*u*   -less flavor

Ile – how much, how many
    ile pienięd*zy*? -how much money?

Bez – without
      bez cukr*u*   -without sugar

Kilo masł*a*   -A kilogram of butter
Deko ser*a*   -A decogram of cheese
Litr mlek*a*   -A liter of milk

• **ADJECTIVES AND POSSESSIVE PRONOUNS**

As discussed earlier, adjectives and most possessive pronouns must agree with the nouns they modify in gender and case. Adjectives in the genitive are quite regular.

-Masculine –**ego**:
tego	dobrego
ostrego	długiego
wysokiego	taniego
głupiego	waszego

-Feminine –**ej**:
tej	dobrej
ostrej	długiej
wysokiej	taniej
głupiej	waszej

-Neuter –**ego**:
tego	dobrego
ostrego	długiego
wysokiego	taniego
głupiego	waszego

• ***UWAGA!!* DECLENSION OF NAMES**

Names in Polish are treated as any other noun. Therefore, for the most part, men's names will end in a consonant, and women's names will end in an "a." As nouns they will decline according to case as other nouns. For example:

-Nom: Adam widzi kota   -Adam sees a cat.
-Acc: (Ja) Widzę Adama.   -I see Adam.
-Gen: To jest dom Adama .   -This is Adam's house.

-Nom: Ewa ma córkę.   -Ewa has a daughter.
-Acc: Jan zna Ewę.   - Jan knows Ewa.
-Gen: (Oni) Nie znają Ewy.   -They don't know Ewa.

Some last names act like adjectives rather than nouns. As adjectives they will agree with the first name in gender and case. For example:

Nom. Adam Janowski
     Ewa Janowska
Acc. Adama Janowskiego
     Ewę Janowską
Gen. Adama Janowskiego
     Ewy Janowskiej

In the above examples Adam and Ewa could be husband and wife. Though their last names look different they are actually the same last name. The "*ski*" ending is for the man, while the "*ska*" ending is for the woman.

If a last name looks like a noun it will decline like a noun for a man, but will not change for a woman. For example:

Nom. Adam Nowak
     Ewa Nowak
Acc. Adama Nowaka
     Ewę Nowak
Gen. Adama Nowaka
     Ewy Nowak

• **PERSONAL PRONOUNS**

Nom.	Gen.
ja	mnie
ty	ciebie
on	go / (dla) niego
ona	jej / (dla) niej
ono	go / (dla) niego
pan	pana
pani	pani
my	nas
wy	was
oni	ich / (dla) nich

• **QUESTIONS** in the genitive would be formed according to the following examples:

Kogo szukasz?	-Who are you looking for?
Do kogo idziesz?	-(To) Who(m) are you going (to see)?
Od kogo to masz?	-From whom do you have that?
Czego się uczysz?	-What are you learning?
Czego nie lubisz?	-What don't you like?
Jakiej muzyki słuchasz?	-What kind of music do you listen to?
Jakiego długopisu używasz?	-What kind of pen do you use?
Do którego miasta jedziesz?	-Which city are you going to?

Której książki nie czytasz?	-Which book are you not reading?
Do czyjego domu idziecie?	-Whose house are you going to?
Dla czyjej siostry kupisz róży?	-For whose sister will you buy roses?

Exercise 7: Rewrite the following sentences according to the example. Look up any vocabulary you don't know. Remember that words like "*mój*" "*twój*" "*swój*" "*ten*" "*ta*" "*to*" decline like adjectives.

• Moja siostra ma mieszkanie. <u>To jest mieszkanie mojej siostry</u>.

1: Anna ma psa. _____.

2: Tę książkę napisał Bolesław Prus. _____.

3: Joanna Mizielińska napisała ten artykuł. _____.

4: Jan ma psa. _____.

5: Ten samochód kupił mój ojciec. _____.

6: Ten dom kupiła moja matka. _____.

Exercise 8: Rewrite the sentences according to the example. Be sure to decline both the adjectives and nouns:

• Adam lubi piwo. <u>Adam nie lubi piwa</u>.

1: On pije mocną kawę. _____.

2: Oni lubią tę polską piosenkę. _____.

3: Agnieszka zna profesora Czaplinskiego. _____.

4: Mirek studiuje filologię angielską. _____.

5: Chcemy kupić ten nowy komputer. _____.

Exercise 9: Complete the sentences following the example:

•Szukam _____ (swój długopis). <u>Szukam swojego długopisu.</u>

1: Szukam _____ (swoja książka).

2: Lubię słuchać _____ (nowoczesna muzyka).

3: Uczę się _____ (język polski).

4: Ja tylko potrzebuję _____ (mały słownik).

5: Szukamy _____ (dobre piwo).

Exercise 10: Complete the following sentences according to the example. Look up any new vocabulary: •Idę do __<u>domu</u>__ (dom).

1: Wieczorem idziemy do _____ (moja babcia).

2: Do _____ idziecie? (kto)

3: Anna mieszka teraz u _____ (ciotka).

4: To jest rower dla _____ (mój brat).

5: Jesteśmy tutaj od _____ (poniedziałek).

•INSTRUMENTAL: KIM? CZYM? KIMŚ, CZYMŚ

Unfortunately, English does not have an equivalent of the **instrumental** (*narzędnik*) case. However, it is a very regular case. The *Instrumental* is used in 3 circumstances.

•MASCULINE NOUNS
Masculine nouns that end in consonants take the ending "*-em.*"

- -studentem
- -ojcem
- -autobusem
- -długopisem
- -domem
- - prezydentem
- -Markiem
- -lekarzem

Masculine nouns that end in "*a*" take the ending "*-ą.*"

- -poetą
- -kierowcą
- -mężczyzną
- -turystą

•FEMININE NOUNS
All feminine nouns take the ending ""*-ą.*"

- -Ewą
- -dziewczyną
- -kawą
- -powieścią
- -rakietą
- -kobietą
- -lekarką
- -rzeczą
- -herbatą
- -miłością

•NEUTER NOUNS
All neuter nouns take the ending "*-em.*"
- -piwem
- -oknem
- -mieszkaniem
- -winem
- -dzieckiem
- -piórem

•PREPOSITIONS
The first use of the instrumental is after certain prepositions.

"Z"
When used with the instrumental, "z" does not mean "from" as after the *genitive*, but instead means "*with.*"

Rozmawiam z Janem.	-I'm speaking with Jan.
Idę z Anną.	-I'm going with Anna.
Zawsze widzę go z piwem.	-I always see him with a beer.

"Przed"
When used with the instrumental, "*przed*" means "before" or "in front of."

Stoi przed budynkiem. -He's standing in front of the building.
Oglądam wiadomości przed kolacja. -I watch the news before dinner.

"Za"
When used with the instrumental, "*za*" means "after" or "behind."

Słyszę coś za tąścianą. -I hear something behind that wall.
Pójdę za tobą. -I'll go after you.

"Pod"
When used with the instrumental, "*pod*" means "under."

Kot leży pod stołem. -The cat is lying under the table.
Ona mieszka pode mną. -She lives under me.

"Nad"
When used with the instrumental, "*nad*" means "above," or "over."

Są chmury nad morzem. -There are clouds above the sea.
Zdjęcie wisi nad kanapa. -The picture is hanging above the couch.

"*Nad*" can also mean "at" when talking about bodies of water.

Będziemy nad morzem latem. -We'll be at the seaside in the summer.
Lubię siedzić nad rzeką. -I like to sit beside the river.

"Między"
When used with the instrumental, "między" means "between," or "among."

Jest między stołem a kanapą. -It's between the table and couch.
 Są zdrajcy między nami! -There are traitors among us!

- **"BY MEANS OF"**

The seond reason we use the instrumental is without "z" in order to express "**with**" or "**by means of**." Look at the following examples:

Jadę samochodem. -I'm going by car.
Pisze długopisem. -She's writing with a pen.
Jesteśmy pijani wódką. -We're drunk on vodka.
Rozmrażać mikrofalówka. -Thaw with a microwave.
Czy kopiesz łopatą? -Are you digging with a shovel?

•*UWAGA!!* Though this may seem rather difficult to grasp, it actually comes quite naturally. Be sure not to confuse this second reason with the first. For example, if you want to express "I'm writing with a pen" do not use "z." The preposition "z" only expresses what is with someone, not what someone is using.

•BEING

The third reason the instrumental is used is a bit more difficult. It is used when we express "what" someone is. For example:

Pan Nowicki jest lekarzem.	-Mr. Nowicki is a doctor.
Będę nauczycielem.	-I will be a teacher.
Pani Nowicka jest lekarką.	-Ms. Nowicka is a (female) doctor.
Moja matka jest nauczycielką.	-My mother is a (female) teacher.
Ona była studentką.	-She was a student.
On jest studentem.	-He is a student.
Ona jest moją siostrą.	-She is my sister.
On jest moim bratem.	-He is my brother.
Jestem Amerykaninem.	-I'm an American (man).
Jestem Amerykanką.	-I'm an American (woman).

As we can see, the instrumental in this circumstance is used after "to be," quite often telling us what someone's career is. But as we see in the last two examples, we use it after "to be" simply to express what someone is. However, the instrumental is not only used with people. For example:

Mój samochód jest wielkim problemem.	-My car is big problem.
Moja kochana jest czerwoną różą.	-My love is a red rose.
Oko jest oknem ducha.	-The eye is a window of the soul.

• USE OF "TO"

In colloquial Polish you will quite often hear people use "*to*" in the above examples without "*jest*" and without declining the noun in the instrumental. For example:

On to lekarz.
Ona to studentka.
Mój samochód to wielki problem.
Moja kochana to czerwona róża.
Oko to okno ducha.

As we can see, there is no verb in the above sentences. This is a common feature in some Slavic languages, which can also be seen in Russian where "to be" is not even conjugated in the present tense. (If one wanted to say in Russian "I am a teacher" it would be something like "I teacher.") Though this is not incorrect it is a more informal way of speaking, and you will not encounter it as often in writing as you will in speech.

- **INTERESOWAĆ SIĘ**

Just as there are certain verbs that must use the *genitive*, so too there are certain verbs that must use the *instrumental*. One of the most common of these is "*interesować się*" "to be interested in something." In order to express this we must first conjugate the verb, and then use the instrumental to say what it is one is interested in. For example:

Interesuję się językiem polskim.   -I'm interested in the Polish language.
Interesuje się kulturą hiszpańską.   -She's interested in Spanish culture.
Interesował się samochodem.   -He was interested in the car.

- **Personal pronouns**

Nom.	Inst.
ja	mną
ty	tobą
on	nim
ona	nią
ono	nim
pan	panem
pani	panią
my	nami
wy	wami
oni	nimi

- **QUESTIONS** in the instrumental would be formed as follows.

Kim on jest?   -Who (What) is he?
Z kim idziesz do kina?   -With whom are you going to the cinema?
Czym naprawiasz samochód?   -What will you fix the car with?
Z czym tam stoisz?   -What are you standing there with?
Jakim dlugopisem pisze?   -With what kind of pen is she writing?
Z jaką torebką idzie?   -With what kind of purse is she walking?
Którym autobusem jadą?   -Which bus are they taking?
Z którą flagą maszerujesz?   -With which flag are you marching?
Czyim samochodem jedziecie?   -Whose car are you taking to work?
Z czyją siostrą idziesz?   -Whose sister are you going with?
Czym interesujesz się?   -What are you interested in?

- **Adjectives and Possessive Pronouns**

Adjectives decline in the following ways in the *instrumental*.

Masculine: -ym –im:
tym   dobrym
ładnym   długim
wysokim   tanim
głupim   waszym

Feminine: -ą:
tą   dobrą
ładną   długą
wysoką   tanią
głupią   waszą

Neuter: -ym –im:
tym   dobrym
ładnym   długim
wysokim   tanim
głupim   waszym

Exercise 11: Complete the following sentences according to the example. Look up any new vocabulary.
• Jósef jest ___starym Polakiem_____ (stary Polak).

1: Adam jest _____ (młody Amerykanin).

2: Jenny jest _____ (młoda Amerykanka).

3: _____ był Jacques Chirac (Kto) ?

4: Jacques Chirac był _____ (prezydent) Francji.

5: Agata jest _____ (lekarka).

6: Ireniusz jest _____ (lekarz).

Exercise 12: Complete the following sentences according to the example.
• Z kim rozmawia (kto)?
1: Kot leży pod _____ (stół).

2: Ptak leci nad _____ (drzewo).

3: Poczta stoi między _____ a _____ (sklep, biblioteka).

4: Przed _____ jest ładny park (nasze mieszkanie).

5: Za _____ jest parking (budynek).

Exercise 13: Complete the following sentences according to the example.
• Czym jedziesz do Nowego Jorku (Co)?
1: Ja zawsze jeżdżę do pracy _____ (autobus).

2: Pojedziemy do Kanady _____ (pociąg).

3: Lecą do Polski _____ (samolot).

4: Wolę pisać _____ (długopis).

•LOCATIVE: O KIM? O CZYM? O KIMŚ, O CZYMŚ

Though English does not have an equivalent to the **locative** (*miejscownik*) case, it is actually quite easy since one only ever uses it after certain prepositions; *na* (on), *o* (about), *w* (in), *przy* (next to), *po* (after).

•Nouns

It is simply necessary to memorize the way nouns change in the locative case. One can achieve this by remembering how the *final consonants* of nouns change. As you will see, the system of declination seems rather arbitrary, but it's actually not that difficult to memorize. Most endings illustrate a softening (**palatalization**) of the final consonant with the addition of the front vowel "*e*." For example, when the "*ł*" of "*stół*" is palatalized by adding "*e*" the "*ł*" must change to an "*l*." Or when the "*r*" of "*literatura*" is palatalized it must become a "*rze*" or "**zh**" sound. But instead of trying to figure this out, the following graph will make the memorization of the *final consonant* changes much easier.

Locative Endings

b – bie	f – fie	**k – ku**	m – mie	r – rze	w – wie	**rz – rzu**
ba – bie	fa – fie	**ka – ce**	ma – mie	ra – rze	wa – wie	**sz – szu**
bo – bie	fo – fie	**ko – ku**	mo – mie	ro – rze	wo – wie	**cz – czu**
c – cu	g – gu	l – lu	n – nie	s – sie	z – zie	**ia – i**
ca – cy	ga – dze	la – le	na – nie	sa – sie	za – zie	-or-
co – cu	go – gu	lo – lu	no – nie	so – sie	zo – zie	**ia – ii**
d – dzie	j – ju	ł – le	p – pie	t – cie	ż – żu	ie – iu
da – dzie	ja – ji	ła – le	pa – pie	ta – cie	ża – ży	sta – ście
do – dzie	jo – ju	ło – le	po – pie	to – cie	żo – żu	sto – ście

UWAGA!! You will notice that the "*ia*" ending can become "*i*" or "*ii*." There are many feminine nouns that end with "*-ia*," and many of these are borrowed words. If it is originally a Polish word, such as "*babcia*" the locative will simply drop the "*a*" and become "*o babci*." If it is a borrowed word, such as country names like "*Anglia*," the locative will be formed by changing the "*a*" to "*i*," becoming "*w Anglii*."

You will also notice the sections of the graph that are in **bold**. These are the only exceptions to the "*e*" ending in the locative.

"**Na**" means "on." As we saw earlier, "*na*" can also be used in the *accusative* case, but when used thus it implies motion. For example:

Jade na Kubę.   -I'm going (on)to Cuba.

Since it is an island, we have to go "onto" Cuba. If, however, we are already in Cuba we would have to use the *locative*, which implies **stasis**. For example:

Jestem na Kubie.   -I'm in (on) Cuba.

"**O**" is used when we want to express "about" what or whom we know or are talking, reading, thinking, etc. For example:

Mówimy o sztuce.	-We're talking about art.
Nic nie wiem o Meksyku.	-I don't know anything about Mexico.
Ewa czyta o literaturze.	-Ewa is reading about literature.
Często myślę o Polsce.	-I often think about Poland.

"**W**" means "inside." Again, as with "*na*," "*w*" means that something is already inside something else. For example:

Jestem w szkole.	-I'm in school.
Jedzą w restauracji.	-They're eating in the resaturant.
Książka leży na stole.	-The book is lying on the table.
Już jestem w łóżku.	-I'm already in bed.

"**PRZY**" means "next to." For example:

Motocykl stoi przy ścianie.	-The motorcycle's standing next to the wall.
Będę czekał przy budynku.	-I'll be waiting by the building.
Adam siedzi przy Ewie.	-Adam is sitting next to Ewa.

"**PO**" means 'after' in reference to time. For example:

Już jest po pierwszej!	-It's already past one!
Idę do domu po obiedzie.	-I'm going home after lunch.
Po pracy jedziemy do baru.	-After work we're going to the bar.

•ADJECTIVES AND POSSESSIVE PRONOUNS

Masculine: -ym –im:
dobrym	ładnym
ostrym	długim
wysokim	tanim
głupim	moim

Feminine: -ej:
dobrej	ładnej
ostrej	długiej
wyskokiej	taniej
głupiej	mojej

Neuter: -ym –im:
dobrym	ładnym
ostrym	długim
wysokim	tanim
głupim	moim

• **PERSONAL PRONOUNS**

Nom	Loc.
ja	mnie
ty	tobie
on	nim
ona	niej
ono	nim
pan	panie
pani	pani
my	nas
wy	was
oni	nich

• **QUESTIONS**

O kim mówicie?	-About whom are you talking?
O czym myślisz?	-About what are you thinking?
Na którym budynku jest zegar?	-On which building is the clock?
O jakiej książce mówisz?	-About what kind of book are you talking?
Przy czyim krześle stoisz?	-Next to hose chair are you standing?

Exercise 14: Complete the following sentences according to the example.

• Rozmawiamy o <u>filmie</u> (film).

1: W _____ jest wino (ta butelka).

2: Wczoraj, byłam na _____ z profesorem (zebranie).

3: Musiał leżeć w _____ przez dwa dni (łóżko).

4: Po _____ pójdę na spacer (obiad).

5: Mieszkam w _____ przy _____Chuczyńskich (Kraków, pałac).

6: Chcę iść po _____ (ten ładny las).

7: Co czytasz w _____ (gazeta)?

8: O _____ mówicie (kto)?

9: Dlaczego ten kot leży na _____ (mój stół)?

10: Będę czekała na ciebie w _____(restauracja).

•DATIVE: KOMU? CZEMU? KOMUŚ, CZEMUŚ

English uses a kind of **dative** (*celownik*) case, but it is expressed as the **indirect object**. This is the object of the direct object. For example:

-I gave the ball to the dog.

In this sentence "I" is the subject, "ball" is the direct object, and "(to the) dog" is the indirect object. The sentence would be translated as:

-Dałem piłkę ps*u*.

In the one word "*psu*" there is expressed "to the dog." The English sentence can also be written as:

-I gave the dog the ball.

with no change in meaning:

-Dałem ps*u* piłkę.

The *dative* is also often used in place of the preposition "for" in English. For example:

Kupuję t*ej* dziewczyn*ie* piwo.	-I'm buying that girl a beer.
Zrobię *ci* to.	-I'll do it for you.
Gotuję kolację Jack*owi*.	-I'm cooking lunch for Jacek.
Powiem Ann*ie* żart.	-I'll tell a joke to Anna/I'll tell Anna a joke.
Czy pomożesz *mi*?	-Will you help me?
Chcę dzieck*u* pokazać zdjęcie.	-I want to show the child a picture.
Przyglądam się t*emu* zegark*u*.	-I'm having a look at that watch.

As you can see in the above examples, quite often a sentence must have a direct object in order to have an indirect object, as in "I'm cooking lunch for Jacek." However, this is not always the case, and some verbs in Polish simply must have the dative case after it, as in "Will you help me?" "*Pomóc*" ['To Help'] will always need the dative, the indirect object. "*Przyglądać się*" ['Watch, Observe'] also takes the dative for its object.

UWAGA!! Never use the preposition "*do*" [to] in order to express the dative. For example:

WRONG:	-Dałem piłkę do psa.
CORRECT:	-Dałem piłkę psu.

"*Do*" is only used in expressing a verb of motion (see the section on the *genitive* case).

•Masculine Nouns

There are two possible endings for masculine; "-*u*" and "-*owi*." Unfortunately there are few hard and fast rules one can memorize in order to remember which take –*u* and which take –*owi*. **Men's names will almost always take** –*owi*.

Marek   -Dałem Markowi....
Adam   -Dałem Adamowi...
Dawid   -Dałem Dawidowi...

One exception is the name "*Jerzy*," which delines like an adjective.

Jerzy   -Dałem Jerzemu....

Very often **masculine gendered professions** will also take –*owi*:

nauczyciel   – nauczycielowi
prezydent   – prezydentowi
pisarz   – pisarzowi

However, many other words for men will end in –*u*:

ojciec   – ojcu
brat   – bratu
ksiądz   – księdzu
pan   – panu
chłopiec – chłopcu

Unfortunately, those are the only real definite rules that can be followed for masculine nouns. In the beginning you will have to use your dictionary to determine whether the masculine takes –*u* or –*owi*.

kot – kotu   pies–psu
budynek–budynkowi stół–stołowi
dom–domowi

Generally speaking, a masculine noun will most often end in "–*owi*" than "–*u*." So if you need to take a guess, guess "–*owi*."

•Feminine Nouns

Feminine nouns are much easier to figure out as they always decline according to the *locative* case (see the locative graph on page   ).

Muszę pomóc matce.   -I have to help mother.
Dam Annie podarunek.   -I'm going to give Anna a present.
Pokażę babci mój samochód. -I'll show grandma my car.

•Neuter Nouns
Neuter nouns are also easier as they will always take –*u* as their ending.

Kupię dziecku kolę.	-I'll buy the child a cola.
Da miastu jego pracę.	-He'll give the city his work.

•"Ku"
There is one preposition that uses the dative. This is 'ku' ['towards']. It is rather bookish, used rarely in colloquial Polish, but you will come across it in written texts.

Jadę ku morzu.	-I'm going to the sea.
Samolot leci ku niebu.	-The plane is flying towards the sky.
Ku mojemu zdziwieniu...	-To my surprise....

•Common idiomatic expressions
There are some common Polish idioms that use the dative. For example:

dzięki komu/czemu	-thanks to someone/something
Dzięki tobie, mam pracę.	-Thanks to you, I have a job.
Dzięki śniegowi, nie ma szkoły.	-Thanks to snow there is no school.

We have already seen how to use the verb "*lubić*" to express "to like." However, "*lubić*" is quite strong, and a more common expression you will come across is "*podobać się komuś*," literally meaning "to be pleasing to someone."

Podoba mi się ona.	-I like her (She is pleasing to me).
Czy podoba ci się szkoła?	-Do you like the school?
Jak wam się podobają buty?	-How do you all like the shoes?

As you can see, the thing "being enjoyed" is actually the **subject** of the sentence. So in the second example "Is the school pleasing to you," the "to you" is expressed in "*ci*." In the third sentence the "*buty*" are pleasing ["*podobają się*"] to you all ["*wam*"].

Another important idiom is how Polish expresses external states affecting a person. For example, to express that you are cold in Polish it would be incorrect to say:

Jestem zimny.   -I am cold

This literally means that you are eminating coldness from your body. To correctly express this you would say

Jest mi zimno.   -Literally: It is cold to/for me.

Similarly, to express that your are hot you would say:

Jest mi ciepło.   -It is warm for me.

not:
Jestem ciepły.   -I am warm.

You would only say the second sentence if you had a fever, and indeed your skin were <u>actually</u> warm. This is also the construction we would use to express comfort. If we say:

Jestem wygodny.   -I am comfortable.

this actually means that you have the qualities of a couch, and people enjoy sitting on you. The following sentences illustrate the proper construction.

Czy to krzesło jest ci wygodne?   -Is the chair comfortable for you?
Jest mi wygodne.   -It is comfortable for me.

•Questions

Komu dasz ten zegarek?   -To whom are you giving that watch?
Czemu się przyglądasz?   -What are you looking at?
Któremu kotu mam dać jeść?   -Which cat am I supposed to feed?
Jakiej książce się przygląda?   -What kind of book is he looking at?
Czyjemu bratu pomożesz?   -Whose brother are you helping?

•ADJECTIVES AND POSSESSIVE PRONOUNS

Masculine: -emu:
dobremu   ładnemu
ostremu   długiemu
wysokiem   taniemu
głupiemu   mojemu

Feminine: -ej:
dobrej   ładnej
ostrej   długiej
wyskokiej   taniej
glupiej   mojej

Neuter: -emu:
dobremu   ładnemu
ostremu   długiemu
wysokiemu   taniemu
głupiemu   mojemu

•Personal pronouns

Nom	Dat.
ja	mi
ty	ci/tobie
on	mu / jemu
ona	jej / niej
ono	mu / jemu
pan	panu
pani	pani
my	nam
wy	wam
oni	im / nim

Exercise 15: Complete the following sentences according to the example:

• <u>Komu</u> pomożesz? (kto)

1: Co dałeś _____ (mama)?

2: Jeden student dał _____ prezent. (profesor)

3: Czy powiesz _____ o tym (ojciec)?

4: Czy jest _____ za zimno (ty)?

5: Ale! Ona bardzo _____ się podoba (ja)!!

6: Dzięki _____ mogę pójść na koncert (ona).

7: _____ przyglądasz się (co)?

8: Pokazamy _____ nasze zdjęcia (Jan).

9: Czy możecie _____ pożyczyć te książki (my)?

10: Dzięki _____ zdałem mój egzamin (wasza pomoc).

•VOCATIVE: KTO? CO? KTOŚ, COŚ

The vocative case is both the easiest and least used of the cases. It is used when speaking to someone, or calling to them. For example:

Anno, możesz tu przyjść? -Anna, can you come here?
Dawidzie! Przystań to! -David! Stop that!

The vocative is quite often found in poetry in place of the "Oh!" of English. Look at this example from the opening of the famous poem "Pan Tadeusz" by Adam Mickiewicz.

"Litwo! Ojczyzno moja!" -"Oh Lithuania! Oh my homeland!"

The vocative case is used less and less in contemporary Polish, but it is still important to learn it. The masculine form of the vocative is the same as the locative.

Stole! -Oh table!
Jacku! -Oh Jacek!
Adamie! -Oh Adam!
Boże! -Oh God!

Feminine nouns that end in an "a" will simply change to an "o."

Katarzyno! -Oh Katarzyna!
Książko! -Oh book!
Litwo! -Oh Lithuania!
Polsko! -Oh Poland!

Feminine nouns that end in a consonant is the same as the genitive.

Powieści! -Oh novel!
Rzeczy! -Oh thing!

Neuter nouns do not change in the vocative.

Piwo! -Oh beer!

•**Adjectives and Possessive Pronouns** in the vocative do not change from the nominative case.

5: PLURALITY

Now that we have seen all the cases in their singular forms we can move onto their plural forms. Fortunately, although nouns do have different forms in the plural, there is nothing new to learn about their function in the sentence. If a noun in the singular accuastive is the direct object of the sentence, more than one of the same noun is still going be the direct object.

•NUMBERS; CARDINAL

Before discussing plural nouns we should get acquainted with numbers, without which there would be no plurality.

1 jeden, jedna, jedno	31 trzydzieści jeden
2 dwa, dwie	40 czterdzieści
3 trzy	50 pięćdziesiąt
4 cztery	60 sześćdziesiąt
5 pięć	70 siedemdziesiąt
6 sześć	80 osiemdziesiąt
7 siedem	90 dziewięćdziesiąt
8 osiem	100 sto
9 dziewięć	101 sto jeden
10 dziesięć	200 dwieście
11 jedenaście	300 trzysta
12 dwanaście	400 czterysta
13 trzynaście	500 pięćset
14 czternaście	600 sześćset
15 piętnaście	700 siedemset
16 szesnaście	800 osiemset
17 siedemnaście	900 dziewięćset
18 osiemnaście	1000 tysiąc
19 dziewiętnaście	2000 dwa tysiąca
20 dwadzieścia	5000 pięć tysięcy
21 dwadzieścia jeden	10,000 dziesięć tysięcy
22 dwadzieścia dwa	100,000 sto tysięcy
23 dwadzieścia trzy	1,000,000 milion
30 trzydzieści	1,000,000,000 miliard

As you can see, the numbers 1 and 2 have more than one form. "*Jeden, jedna, jedno*" act similarly to "*ten, ta, to,*" declining like adjectives. "*Dwa*" is used for masculine and neuter, while "*dwie*" is used for feminine nouns.

Numbers will all decline according to case. Their changes will be illustrated in the following sections.

•Numbers; Ordinal

Ordinal numbers are the counting numbers, such as "first," "second," and "third." In Polish, these numbers take the form of **adjectives** in **gender** and **case**. This means that they will take all the endings that normal adjectives take in the same circumstances.

1st	pierwsz*y* / *a* / *e*	20th	dwudziesty
2nd	drug*i* / *a* / *ie*	30th	trzydziesty
3rd	trzec*i* / *ia* / *ie*	40th	czterdziesty
4th	czwart*y* / *a* / *e*	50th	pięćdziesiąty
5th	piąt*y* / *a* / *e*	60th	sześćdziesiąty
6th	szóst*y* / *a* / *e*	70th	siedemdziesiąty
7th	siódm*y* / *a* / *e*	80th	osiemdziesiąty
8th	ósmy	90th	dziewięćdziesiąty
9th	dziewiąty	100th	setny
10th	dziesiąty	200th	dwusetny
11th	jedenasty	300th	trzechsetny
12th	dwunasty	400th	czterechsetny
13th	trzynasty	500th	pięćsetny
14th	czternasty	600th	sześćsetny
15th	piętnasty	700th	siedemsetny
16th	szesnasty	800th	osiemsetny
17th	siedemnasty	900th	dziewięćsetny
18th	osiemnasty	1000th	tysięczny
19th	dziewiętnasty	2000th	dwutysięczny

•NOMINATIVE PLURAL

As in the singular, the nominative plural is the subject of the sentence. Instead of using the singular person conjugation of verbs, we must now use the plural person conjugations. An important point to keep in mind is that in the plural there are the designations **"virile"** and **"non-virile."** This means "men" and "everything else."

Dwa długopisy leżą na stole. -Two pens are lying on the table.
Dwie książki są w moim plecaku. -Two books are in my bag.
Trzy psy jedzą kość. -Three dogs are eating a bone.
Są cztery okna. -There are four windows.

As you can see, forming plural nouns is not that difficult.

•**MASCULINE** *inanimate* and *non-virile* (not men) nouns take a '"y" or "i" ending to make the nominative plural.

długopisy	ołówki	psy
koty	domy	stoły
skarpetki	kubki	

If masculine nouns end in "cz," "rz," or "l" the plural ending would be "e."

klucze
bale
kurze

•**FEMININE** nouns also change the ending to 'y' or 'i' to make the nominative plural. For feminine nouns this is the same form as the **genitive** singular.

książki	kobiety	powieści
nauczycielki	żaby	szkoły
rzeczy		

•**NEUTER** nouns change their endings to 'a' in order to form the nominative plural. As with feminine nouns, this is also the **genitive** singular for neuter.

| okna | mieszkania | piwa |
| jedzenia | pióra | krzesła |

Neuter nouns that end in"-*um*" also takes the "a" ending in the nominative plural.

muzea   centra

•Plural Adjectives and Possessive Pronouns – Non-Virile

The adjectives for these nouns in the plural would have the same ending as singular neuter nouns, "-*e*." For example:

masculine
dwa dobre długopisy   trzy ładne psy   cztery niskie stoły
te drogie samochody   moje klucze

feminine
dwie dobre książki   trzy ładne kobiety cztery niskie szkoły
te drogie rzeczy   moje ulicy

neuter
dwa dobre okna   trzy ładne muzea   cztery niskie krzesła
te drogie mieszkania   moje pióra

•Plural Virile Masculine Nouns

Unfortunately, when making **virile masculine** nouns (men only) plural, there are some seemingly arbitrary systems at play. Some simply take the ending "-*owie*." This is usually for masculine **familial** nouns, nouns that show some kind of **high rank**, and **last names** that do not end with -*ski* or -*cki*. For example:

professor – profesorowie   pan - panowie
syn – synowie   szef – szefowie
ojciec – ojcowie   generał – generałowie
mąż - mężowie   doktor – doktorowie
dziadek – dziadkowie   Nowak – Nowakowie
wujek - wujkowie   Sienkiewicz – Sienkiewiczowie
król – królowie   Mickiewicz – Mickiewiczowie

UWAGA!! Note that to say "grandpa and grandma" one would use the plural for "grandpa," "*dziadkowie*." Plural last names, such as "*Nowakowie*," imply "Mr. and Mrs. Nowak."

The true difficulty of the nominative plural comes in figuring out how to make other virile nouns plural. Some quick linguistic jargon may be helpful. When pluralizing virile nouns, except for the above exceptions, one must simply add an "-*i*." However, this addition of the **front** vowel **palatalizes** (softens) the **final** consonant, which changes its character. For example, the noun "*prezydent*" ends with a "*t*." When it is **palatalized** the "*t*" becomes a "*ć*." Since it must be followed by an "*i*" the ending becomes "*ci*." Therefore "presidents" in Polish would be "*prezydenci*." However, the noun "*Polak*" ends with "*k*."

When **palatalized** "k" becomes a "c." Unlike the "ć" in "*prezydenci*" the "c" must continue to sound like "*ts*." Therefore it must end in a "-*y*." So "Poles" in Polish would be "*Polacy*." Look at the following consonants for the changes they undergo.

b – bie	f – fie	ł – li	p – pie	t – ci
ch – si	g – dzy	m – mie	r – rzy	w – fie
d – dzi	k – cy	n – nie	s – si	z – zi

For example:

Włoch   – Włosi
student – studenci
Anglik   – Anglicy
kolega   – koledzy
Amerykanin – Amerykanie
poeta   – poeci

Other endings are already considered soft, such as "*rz*," "*cz*," and "*l*." The plural for these would be "e," similarly to non-virile nouns that end in the same way.

lekarz   – lekarze
nauczyciel – nauczyciele
gracz   – gracze
pisarz   – pisarze
obywatel – obywatele

• VIRILE PLURAL ADJECTIVES AND POSSESSIVE PRONOUNS
A **palatalization** similar to what we find in virile nouns also occurs in the adjectives that modify virile nouns. The following graph illustrates this softening:

Sg	by	dy	chy	gi	ki	ły	my	ny	py	ry	sy	szy	ty	wy	ży
Pl	bi	dzi	si	dzy	cy	li	mi	ni	pi	rzy	si	si	ci	wi	zi

This graph illustrates that when, for example, an adjective in the singular ends in "-*dy*," like "*młody*," the plural for **virile** nouns will end in "-*dzi*," "*młodzi*." Thus, the possessive pronoun "*mój*" in the **virile** plural would be "*moi*," and "*nasz*" would be "*nasi*."

When the original adjectival form already ends in "-*i*" it stays the same when describing plural virile nouns:

Głupi mężczyzna.   -Stupid man.
Głupi mężczyźni.   -Stupid men.

- **PLURAL EXCEPTIONS**

Common masculine exceptions to the above include "*bracia*," "brothers," "*goście*," "guests," and "*ludzie*," "people," (the singular would be "*człowiek*," "person).

Common feminine exceptions include words that end in "-*ość*" whose plural is the same as the genitive singular, such as "*powieści*."

Common neuter exceptions include "*dzieci*" "children."

- **NUMBERS**

The numbers used for **non-virile** and **non-collective** nouns are simply the original forms. For example:

Masculine:
dwa długopisy   trzy psy   cztery koty

Feminine:
dwie książki   trzy kobiety   cztery ulicy

Neuter:
dwa piwa   trzy okna   cztery mieszkania

The numbers for **virile** nouns will have an "-*ej*" or "-*aj*" ending. For example:

dwaj bracia   dwaj studenci   trzej lekarze
trzej prezydenci   czterej synowie   czterej ojcowie

The numbers for **collective** nouns, such as "*ludzie*," "*dzieci*," and "*drzwi*" have quite strange forms. For example:

dwoje dzieci   troje ludzie   czworo drzwi
pięcioro dzieci   sześcioro ludzie

- **AMOUNTS AND NOUNS ABOVE 5**

There are **4 things** to remember about plural nouns of 5 and above.

1: Except for collective nouns (*ludzie, dzieci*) whenever there are **5 or more** of something we have to use their **genitive plural** forms for the nouns and adjectives. Even though these nouns will remain the subject of the sentence, they take on the genitive plural case. For example:

Pięć kot*ów* leży na podłodze.   -Five cats are lying on the floor.

2: When the subject of the sentence is plural of 5 or more we must use the **3rd person singular** verb form (*leży*) even though it is a plural subject.

Pięć kotów **leży** na podłodze.

In the past we must use the neuter, 3rd person singular form.

Pięć kotów **leżało** na podłodze.   Five cats were lying on the floor.

3: The truly curious thing about these rules is how it changes throughout the chain of numbers. From 2 - 4 we use the normal **nominative** plural and the 3rd person plural. From 5 - 21 we must use the **genitive** plural form and the 3rd person singular. Then the process starts over. 22 - 24 uses the nominative plural, 25 - 31 uses the genitive plural, 32 - 34 nominative plural, 35 - 41 genitive plural, etc. etc. on to infinity. For example:

Jest 21 ołówków w moim plecaku. -There are 21 pencils in my backpack.
Są 22 ołówki w moim plecaku.   -There are 22 pencils in my backpack.

Pięć kobiet miało zebranie.   -Five women had a meeting.
Cztery kobiety miały zebranie.   -Four women had a meeting.

What we see happening in the above sentences is that the numbers that use the genitive plural in essence become the subject of the sentence. So in the first and third example, the numbers 21 and 5 are the subjects. In the second and fourth examples "*ołówki*" and "*kobiety*" remain the subjects.

4: When the subject of the sentence is **virile plural** their adjectives and Numbers will be the same as in the genitive. For example:

Pięciu dobrych studentów uczy się matematyki.
-Five good students are learning math.

Jest sześciu mądrych profesorów tu.
-There are six smart professors here.

Siedmiu młodych poetów pisze wierszy.
-Seven young poets are writing poems.

Było ośmiu starych pisarzy w księgarni.
-There were eight old writers in the bookstore.

•Interrogative Pronouns

The only change we have to keep in mind with interrogative pronouns is in the case of virile nouns. As in other cases they act like adjectives, and so take on the same change that adjectives do. For example:

Jacy są twoi bracia?	-What are your brothers like?
Którzy lekarze pracują dzisiaj?	-Which doctors are working today?
Czyi dziadkowie tu mieszkali?	-Whose grandparents lived here?

Exercise 16: Complete the sentences by putting the words in ( ) into the nominative plural.
• Na stole leżą dwa <u>jabłka</u> (jabłko).

1: Ile kosztują _____ (ta książka)?

2: ____ dwa _____ należą do Jana (ten, dom).

3: Są cztery _____ w Polsce (duże miasto).

4: _____ dwie _____ zawsz kłócą się (ta, siostra).

5: Dokąd jadą ____ dwa _____ (ten, pociąg)?

Exercise 17: Complete the sentences by putting the words in ( ) into the VIRILE nominative plural.

• <u>Moi bracia</u> mają dzieci (mój, brat).

1: Tu pracują bardzo _____ (dobry profesor).

2: Skąd są _____ (ten Polak)?

3: _____ mieszkają tam (znany aktor).

4: Czy _____ mają samochody (wasz kuzyn)?

5: Jacy są _____ (twój nauczyciel)?

•ACCUSATIVE PLURAL

Luckily, the accusative plural is more regular than the nominative, and indeed maintains many similarities with it.

•MASCULINE NON-VIRILE, FEMININE, AND NEUTER NOUNS
These nouns all decline the same way as they do in the nominative plural.

Mam trzy długopisy.	-I have two pens.
Widzę te dwie dziewczyny.	-I see those two girls.
Czy pijesz takie piwa?	-Do you drink those kinds of beers?

•ADJECTIVES, POSSESSIVE PRONOUNS, AND NUMBERS
The adjectives that modify these nouns remain the same as their nominative plural forms.

Mają dobre długopisy.	-They have good pens.
Czy widzisz te dwie małe książki?	-Do you see those pretty girls?
Mają cztery małe mieszkania.	-They have four small apartments.
Piją dwa piwa.	-They're drinking two beers.

•MASCULINE VIRILE NOUNS
Masculine virile nouns all decline the same way as they do in the **genitive** plural.

Znam tych bratów.	-I know those brothers.
Wybrałem dobrych posłów.	-I chose good representatives.
Lubię profesorów.	-I like the professors.

•ADJECTIVES, POSSESSIVE PRONOUNS, AND NUMBERS
The adjectives that modify masculine virile nouns are the same as their **genitive** plural forms. (see page 63)

Mam dwóch młodych bratów. .	-I have two young brothers.
Znałem pięciu starych prezydentów.	-I knew 5 old presidents.
Czy widzisz tych trzech mężczyzn.	-Do you see those 3 men.

•GENITIVE PLURAL

Luckily, as with the accusative, the genitive plural is much more regular than the nom-inative plural, though there are a couple of exceptions that must be kept in mind.

•MASCULINE NOUNS

Regular masculine nouns, whether **animate** or **inanimate**, **virile** or **non-virile**, take the ending "-ów" in the genitive plural:

psów   kotów   ołówków
domów   ojców   synów

Some common exceptions include:
nauczycieli   pisarzy   lekarzy
obywateli   mężczyzn

•FEMININE NOUNS AND NEUTER NOUNS

Regular feminine and neuter nouns decline in a similar way in the genitive plural. They take on what is called the "**zero ending**," that is, they drop their final vowel. For example:

kobieta -kobiet   książka -książek
kawa -kaw   matka -matek
podłoga -podłóg   piwo -piw
okno -okien   pióro -piór
mieszkanie -mieszkań   prawo -praw

UWAGA!! As you can see in the examples of "książek," "matek," and mieszkań," this **zero ending** creation sometimes demands a slight spelling change, which sometimes helps in pronunciation. As you can tell, it is quite easy to pronounce "kobiet," but it is almost impossible to pronounce "matk" or "książk."

Some exceptions to this would include feminine nouns that end in a consonant, which use their **genitive singular** forms in the genitive plural:

rzecz -rzeczy
powieść -powieści

Two exceptions from the neuter include "muzeum" and "dziecko":

muzeów
dzieci

• AMOUNTS IN THE GENITIVE PLURAL

As we saw in the section on amounts (see page 33), when a noun is preceded by an amount, it must take the **genitive** case. This is also true for plural nouns. However, the meanings of some words of amounts change when we use the plural. For example:

Jest dużo wody.. -There is much (a lot of) water...
But
Jest dużo domów... -There are many (a lot of) houses...

Jest dużo cukru... -There is much (a lot of) sugar....
But
Jest dużo książek.... -There are many (a lot of) books....

As we can see in the above examples, when an amount is followed by uncountable nouns, such as water or sugar, we use the genitive singular. When an amount is followed by countable nouns, such as houses or books, we use the genitive plural. Once again we must use the **3rd person singular** (*jest*) even though we are using plural nouns.

• GENITIVE PLURAL ADJECTIVES AND POSSESSIVE PRONOUNS
The endings for adjectives and possessive pronouns in the genitive plural take either an "**-ich**" or "**-ych**" for **all genders**.

Masculine, Feminine, Neuter: *-ych –ich*:

tych	dobrych	ładnych	ostrych	długich
wysokich	tanich	moich	głupich	waszych

• NUMBERS
Numbers in the genitive plural are the same for every gender.

2 -dwóch	20 -dwudziestu
3 -trzech	30 -trzydziestu
4 -czterech	40 -czterdziestu
5 -pięciu	50 -pięćdziesięciu
6 -sześciu	60 -sześćdziesięciu
7 -siedmiu	70 -siedemdziesięciu
8 -ośmiu	80 -osiemdziesięciu
9 -dziewięciu	90 -dwiewięćdziesięciu
10 -dzeisięciu	100 -stu
11 -jedenastu	200 -dwustu
12 -dwanastu	300 -trzystu
13 -trzynastu	400 -czterystu
14 -czternastu	500 -pięciuset
15 -piętnastu	600 -sześciuset
16 -szesnastu	700 -siedmiuset
17 -siedemnastu	800 -osimiuset
18 -osiemnastu	900 -dziewięciuset
19 -dziewięnastu	1000 -tysięcy

Sentences in the genitive plural that use numbers will be formed according to the following examples:

Jadą do dwóch krajów.   -They're going to two countries.
Szuka dwunastu jajek.   -She's looking for twelve eggs.
Nie czytał tych stu książek.   -He didn't read those hundred books.

Exercise 18: Complete the following sentences by putting the words in () into either the accusative or genitive plural:
•Czy kupisz <u>te książki</u> (ta książka) ?

1: Jan ma trzy _____ (duże mieszkanie).

2: Proszę cztery _____ (małe piwo).

3: Czy czytałaś _____ (ta ciekawa książka)?

4: Ile _____ masz (pies)?

5: Nie kupił _____ (ten nowy but).

6: Czy ona zna _____ trzech _____ (twój, brat)?

7: _____ sześciu _____ jest bardzo znanych (ten, aktor).

8: _____ nie ma na zajęciu dzisiaj (która dziewczyna)?

9: To jest dom _____ (nasi rodzice).

10: Ile _____ czytaliście ostatniego roku (książka)?

•INSTRUMENTAL PLURAL

The instrumental plural marks the end of most difficulties in Polish grammar. We use the instrumental plural for the same reasons as we use the instrumental singular, and there are only two endings we must memorize.

•MASCULINE, FEMININE, AND NEUTER NOUNS
The endings for all nouns in the instrumental plural is "-*ami*."

Idę ze studentami.	-I'm going with the students.
Jadą samochdami.	-They're going by cars.
Mężowie szli żonami.	-The husbands were walking with their wives.
Stoją przed oknami.	-They're standing in front of the windows.
Stoją za domami.	-They're standing behind the houses.

A common exception to this would be for "dzieci," which becomes "*dziećmi*" in the instrumental plural.

•ADJECTIVES AND POSSESSIVE PRONOUNS
The endings for adjectives that modify all plural instrumental nouns will be either "-*ymi*" or "-*imi*."

Idą ze swoimi siostrami.	-They're going with their sisters.
Jadą dużymi autobusami.	-They're going by large buses.
Stoją za białymi domami.	-They're standing behind the white houses.
Idzie z waszymi synami.	-She's going with your sons.

•NUMBERS
Numbers in the instrumental plural would be the following:

2 -dwoma (**fem.** dwiema)	40 -czterdziestoma
3 -trzema	50 -piędziesięcioma
4 -czterema	60 -sześdziesięcioma
5 -pięcioma	70 -siedmdziesięcioma
6 -sześcioma	80 -osiemdziesięcioma
7 -siedoma	90 -dziewiędziesęcioma
8 -osioma	100 -stoma
9 -dziwięcioma	200 -dwustoma
10 -dziesięcioma	300 -trzystoma
11 -jedenastoma	400 -czterystoma
12 -dwanastoma	500 -pięciuset
20 -dwudziestoma	600 -sześciuset
30 -trzydziestoma	•**remaining similar to Gen. Pl.**

Sentences with the instrumental plural when using numbers would be constructed according to the following examples:

Idę z dwoma studentami.   -I'm going with two students.
Napisze list trzema długopisami. -She'll write the letter with three pens.
Poszliśmy z osioma psami.   -We walked with eight dogs.

Exercise 19: Complete the sentences putting the words in () into their instrumental plural forms.

•Maria i Józef są <u>Polakami</u> (Polak).

1: Poszedłem do baru z _____ (mój student).

2: Jechali do Polski _____ i _____ (dwa samoloty, trzy pociągi).

3: „Macbeth" i „Romeo i Julia" są _____ Szekspira (dramat).

4: Wiewiórki stoją pod _____ (drzewo).

5: _____ interesujesz się (Jaki pisarz)?

•LOCATIVE PLURAL

The locative plural is also quite regular, similarly to the instrumental plural.

•Nouns
All nouns, masculine, feminine, neuter, virile, take the ending "-*ach*" in the locative plural.

Mówi o studentach.	-He's talking about the students.
Książki stoją na półkach.	-The books are standing on the shelves.
Jest wino w butelkach.	-There is wine in the bottles.
Mieszkałem przy parkach.	-I lived next to the parks.
Musimy myśleć o dzieciach.	-We must think about the children.
Rozmawiamy po zebraniach.	-We'll talk after the meetings.

•Adjectives and Possessive Pronouns
Adjectives for all nouns take the endings "-*ych*" or "-*ich*."

dobrych	tanich
ładnych	których
jakich	małych
dużych	moich

•Numbers
Numbers in the locative plural take the same forms as their genitive equivalents (see above).

Exercise 20: Complete the sentences by putting the words in ( ) into their plural locative forms.

• Rozmawialiśmy o <u>swoich dziewczynach</u> (swoja dziewczyna).

1: Buty leżą przy _____ (drzwi).

2: W _____ mieszkają dużo Polaków (to miasto).

3: Czy myślisz o _____ (swoj egzamin)?

4: Jej koty śpią na jej _____ (czerwone kanapa).

5: Po _____ chodzi dużo psów (ta ulica).

•DATIVE PLURAL

As with the locative and instrumental plural, the dative plural is very regular.

•Nouns

All nouns in the dative plural take the ending "-*om*."

studentom   dziewczynom
dzieciom   kobietom
muzeom   budynkom

•Adjectives and Possessive Prounouns

Adjectives for all nouns take the endings "-*ym*" and "-*im*" in the dative plural.

dobrym   ładnym
dużym   jakim
którym   małym
wysokim   moim

•Numbers

Numbers in the dative plural take the same forms as their genitive equivalents. (See page 60.)

• Vocative Plural

The vocative plural changes exactly the same way as the nominative plural. See 4.2.

6: FUNCTION WORDS

There are several function words in Polish that, as in English, don't really have much of a meaning but are essential to constructing the language:

-**CZY** has a couple of functions. If it appears at the beginning of a sentence it acts as a marker, letting us know that the sentence will be a "yes/no" question. For example:

Czy znasz Davida?   -Do you know David?
Czy pójdziesz do domu?   -Are you going home?
Czy ona jest lekarką?   -Is she a doctor?

It can also mean "**whether**" or "**if**" when connecting two clauses. For example:

Nie wiem, czy zna mnie.   -I don't know whether/if she knows me.
Nie wie, czy pójdzie.   -She doesn't know if she'll go.

It can also mean "**or**" when there is a choice to be made. For example:

Chcesz kawę czy herbatę?   -Do you want coffee or tea?
Pójdziesz z Anną czy ze mną?   -Are you going with Anna or me?

-**ALBO** also means "**or**," but only as a conjunction with "**either**." For example:

Pojadę albo do Krakowa, albo do Poznania.
-I'll go either to Crakow or Poznan.

Albo chcesz wojnę albo pokój.
-Either you want war or peace.

-**ŻE** means "**that**," but only as a conjunction. Never use "*że*" in the sense of "**that car**," "**that man**," etc. For example:

Wiem, że chcesz pójść.   -I know (that) you want to go.
Czy myślisz, że to jest dobra kawa?   -Do you think (that) this is good coffee?
Skąd wiesz, że boję się psów?   -How do you know (that) I'm afraid of dogs?

-**DLACZEGO** means "**why**?" For example:

Dlaczego pijesz piwo?   -Why are you drinking beer?
Dlaczego musimy pójść?   -Why do we have to go?

-**BO** and **PONIEWAŻ** both mean "**because**," but they will be used in different cir-cumstances. *Ponieważ* can also mean "since." For example:

Bo tak powiedziałem!
-Because I said so!

Ponieważ jestem nowy, nie zarabiam dużo.
-Since I'm new here, I don't make much.

-**DLATEGO** means "**that is why**." For example:

Dlatego nie mogłem wrocić.
-That's why I couldn't come back.

-**ALE** means "**but**." For example:

Chciałem kupić lody, ale matka nie pozwoliła mi.
-I wanted to buy ice cream, but mom wouldn't let me.

-**CHYBA** means "**probably**," but does not carry the same idea of certainty, though it is more certain than "*może*," "**maybe**." For example:

Chyba nie masz czasu.
-You probably don't have time.

-**NA PEWNO** means "**for certain**" or "**certainly**." For example:

Na pewno będziesz chciał więcej tortu.
-You'll certainly want more cake.

-**MOŻE**, when standing alone, means "**maybe**." This is also the 3rd person singular for "*móc*," "**to be able**." For example:

Może znasz tego pana?
-Maybe you know that man?

7• TIME: HOURS, DAYS, MONTHS, YEARS

•TELLING TIME
To talk about the time of day in Polish we have to use the *ordinal* numbers
To ask "What time is it?" in Polish we actually ask "**Which hour is it?**" "*Która jest godzina?*" Poles also use the 24 hr. clock to tell time. So 1pm would be expressed as the "**13th**" "*trzynasta*" hour.

Która jest godzina?	-What time is it?
Jest ósma.	-It's eight o'clock.
Jest już dwudziesta (20:00)!!	-It's already 8pm!
O której (godzinie) pójdziemy do domu?	-At what time are we going home?
Pójdziemy o dziewiętnastej (godzinie)	-We'll go at 7pm.
Koncert zaczyna się o dwudziestej (20:00).	-The concert starts at 8pm

As we can see in the last three examples, in order to express **a time in the future or past** we must use "*o*" for "**at**" and the **locative** case.

•THE DAYS OF THE WEEK
The days of the week are nouns, but only decline in a few instances.

Monday **poniedziałek**	Until Monday **do poniedziałku**	On Monday **w poniedziałek**
Tuesday **wtorek**	Until Tuesday **do wtorku**	On Tuesday **we wtorek**
Wednesday **środa**	Until Wednesday **do środy**	On Wednesday **w środę**
Thursday **czwartek**	Until Thursday **do czwartku**	On Thursday **w czwartek**
Friday **piątek**	Until Friday **do piątku**	On Friday **w piątek**
Saturday **sobota**	Until Saturday **do soboty**	On Saturday **w sobotę**
Sunday **niedziela**	Until Sunday **do niedzieli**	On Sunday **w niedzielę**

As you can see, to say "**until**" a certain day we put the day into the **genitive** after "*do*." To say "**on**" a certain day we use "*w*" and the **accusative**.

- **MONTHS**

Like days, months in Polish are also nouns that must decline in certain circumstances.

	Nom.	Gen.	Loc.
January	**styczeń**	**do stycznia**	**w styczniu**
February	**luty**	**do lutego**	**w lutym**
March	**marzec**	**do marca**	**w marcu**
April	**kwiecień**	**do kwietnia**	**w kwietniu**
May	**maj**	**do maja**	**w maju**
June	**czerwiec**	**do czerwca**	**w czerwcu**
July	**lipiec**	**do lipca**	**w lipcu**
August	**sierpień**	**do sierpnia**	**w sierpniu**
September	**wrzesień**	**do września**	**we wrześniu**
October	**październik**	**do października**	**w październku**
November	**listopad**	**do listopada**	**w listopadzie**
December	**grudzień**	**do grudnia**	**w grudniu**

As we can see in the above graph, similarly to the days of the week we use the **genitive** after "*do*" to express "**until**" a certain month. However, unlike days of the week, we must use the **locative** to express "**in**" a certain month.

- **DATES**

When expressing the date, the day of the month takes the **ordinal** number, followed by the **month**, and both must be in the **genitive**.

Dziewiętnastego stycznia	-The 19th of January
Dwudziestego piątego marca	-The 25th of March
Pierwszego listopada	-The 1st of November

Here, the use of the genitive is quite similar to the English since we must separate the day from the month with "**of**." As the month acts like a noun the day acts like an adjective modifying the noun, and so both must be in the **genitive** case. This idiomatic use of the genitive remains in complete sentences.

Dzisiaj jest poniedziałek, dwunastego listopada.
-Today is Monday, the twelfth of November.

Wczoraj było niedziela, jedenastego listopada.
-Yesterday was Sunday, the eleventh of November.

Jutro będzie wtorek, trzynastego listopada.
-Tomorrow will be Tuesday, the thirteenth of November.

Muszę czekać do środy, czternastego listopada, na nową książkę.
-I have to wait to Wednesday, 14th of November, for a new book.

To talk about years we must place the word "*rok*," "year" before the number.

Rok tysiąc dziewięćset osiemdziesiąty dziewiąty był ważny.
-1989 was an important year.

Urodził się w roku tysiąc dziewięćset pięćdziesiątym czwartym roku.
-He was born in 1954.

Mieszkała tu do dwutysięczny trzeciego roku.
-She lived here until 2003.

As we can see in the above examples, "*rok*" and the numbers of the years must change according to case. The first sentence shows the **nominative**, the second shows the **locative**, and the third sentence shows the **genitive**. What you should notice is that **ONLY** the last two numbers of the year are in the **ORDINAL** and that **ONLY** these numbers change. For example, 1954 is "rok tysiąc dziewięćset pięćdziesiąty czwarty" in the nominative. However, the sentence "He was born *IN* 1954," would become ". . . **w** rok**u** tysiąc dziewięćset pięćdziesią**tym** czwar**tym**," showing the locative changes "u" for the noun (rok, "year") and "ym" for the adjectival ending for the ordinal numbers. The sentence "She lived here *UNTIL* 2003," would become ". . . **do** rok**u** dwutysięczny trzeci**ego**," showing the genitive changes "u" for the noun, and "ego" for the adjective.

Appendix I: Declination Endings for Nouns and Adjectives

- You will find these graphs to be helpful tools while studying Polish. Each box provides the basic changes the endings take according to gender and case.

• Singular Nouns

	Masculine	Feminine	Neuter
Nom.	-consonant (rare) -a	-a (rare) - consonant	-o, -e, -ę, -um
Acc.	Inanimate ---- Animate -no change ---- -a	-ę (rare) - no change	-NO CHANGE
Gen.	-a, -u	-y, -i	-a
Dat.	-owi, -u	-e (**same as Loc. 43**)	-u
Inst.	-em	-ą	-em
Loc.	-e, -u (**see page 43**)	-e (**see page 43**)	-e, -u (**see page 43**)
Voc.	same as Loc.	-o	-No change

• Singular Adjectives

	Masculine	Feminine	Neuter
Nom.	-y	-a	-e
Acc.	Inanimate ---- Animate -y -ego	-ą	-e
Gen.	-ego	-ej	-ego
Dat.	-emu	-ej	-emu
Inst.	-ym	-ą	-ym
Loc.	-ym	-ej	-ym
Voc.	-y	-a	-e

•Plural Nouns

	Masculine	Feminine	Neuter
Nom.	Nonvirile ---- Virile -y, -i ---- -owie -y, -i	-y, -i	-a
Acc.	Nonvirile ---- Virile -y, -i ---- -ów	-y, -i	-a
Gen.	-ów	- drop vowel (rare)-i	-drop vowel
Dat.	-om	-om	-om
Inst.	-ami	-ami	-ami
Loc.	-ach	-ach	-ach
Voc.	-y, -i	-y, -i	-a

•Plural Adjectives

	Masculine	Feminine	Neuter
Nom.	Nonvirile ---- Virile -e ----- -y, -i	-e	-e
Acc.	Nonvirile ---- Virile -e ---- -ych	-e	-e
Gen.	-ych	-ych	-ych
Dat.	-ym	-ym	-ym
Inst.	-ymi	-ymi	-ymi
Loc.	-ach	-ach	-ach
Voc.	-e	-e	-e

Appendix II: Common Polish Verbs

- In the boxes with two verbs, the top verb will be the imperfective and the bottom verb will be the perfective.

INFINITIVE	1ST/2ND PERSON	L FORM	IMPERATIVE	ENGLISH
być	jestem / jesteś	był	Bądź!	to be
mieć	mam / masz	miał	Miej!	to have
wiedzieć	wiem / wiesz	wiedział	Wiedz!	to know
móc	mogę / możesz	mógł		can
mówić	mówię / mówisz	mówił	Mów!	to speak /
powiedzieć	powiem / powiesz	powiedział	Powiedz!	say / tell
chcieć	chcę / chcesz	chciał		to want
musieć	muszę / musisz	musiał		must
prosić	proszę / prosisz	prosił	Proś!	please /
poprosć	poproszę / poprosisz	poprosił	Poproś!	to ask for
myśleć	myślę / myślisz	myślał	Myśl!	to think
pomyśleć	pomyślę / pomyślisz	pomyślał	Pomyśl!	
widzieć	widzę / widzisz	widział		to see
zobaczyć	zobaczę / zobaczysz	zobaczył	Zobacz!	
robić	robię / robisz	robił	Rób!	to do /
zrobić	zrobię / zrobisz	zrobił	Zrób!	to make
iść	idę / idziesz	szedł / szła	Idź!	to go / to
pójść	pójdę / pójdziesz	poszedł/poszła	Pójdź!	walk
chodzić	chodzę / chodzisz	chodził	Chodź!	to go (often)
rozumieć	rozumiem / rozumiesz	rozumiał		to
zrozumieć	zrozumiem / zrozumiesz	zrozumiał	Zrozum!	understand
dawać	daję / dajesz	dawał	Dawaj!	to give
dać	dam / dasz	dał	Daj!	
słyszeć	słyszę / słyszysz	słyszał		to hear
usłyszeć	usłyszę / usłyszysz	usłyszał	Usłysz!	
pamiętać	pamiętam / pamiętasz	pamiętał	Pamiętaj!	to
zapamiętać	zapamiętam / zapamiętasz	zapamiętał	Zapamiętaj!	remember
żyć	żyję / żyjesz	żył	Żyj!	to live
bać się	boję / boisz się	bał się	Bój się!	to be afraid
słuchać	słucham / słuchasz	słuchał	Słuchaj!	to listen
posłuchać	posłucham / posłuchasz	posłuchał	Posłuchaj!	
brać	biorę / bierzesz	brał	Bierz!	to take
wziąć	wezmę / weźmiesz	wziął	Weź!	
czekać	czekam / czekasz	czekał	Czekaj!	to wait
zaczekać	zaczekam / zaczekasz	zaczekał	Zaczekaj!	
zostawać	zostaję / zostajesz	zostawał	Zostawaj!	to stay
zostać	zostanę / zostaniesz	został	Zostań!	
gubić	gubię / gubisz	gubił	Gub!	to lose (an
zgubić	zgubię / zgubisz	zgubił	Zgub!	object)
lubić	lubię / lubisz	lubił		to like
polubić	polubię / polubisz	polubił	Polub!	
patrzyć	patrzę / patrzysz	patrzył	Patrz!	to look at
popatrzyć	popatrzę / popatrzysz	popatrzył	Popatrz!	
siedzieć	siedzę / siedzisz	siedział	Siedź!	to sit
usiąść	usiądę / usiądziesz	usiadł	Usiądź!	
dziękować	dziękuję / dziękujesz	dziękował	Dziękuj!	to thank
podziękować	podziękuję / podziękujesz	podziękował	Podziękuj!	
wychodzić	wychodzę / wychodzisz	wychodził	Wychodź!	to exit
wyjść	wyjdę / wyjdziesz	wyszedł	Wyjdź!	
przepraszać	przepraszam / przepraszasz	przepraszał	Przepraszaj!	to beg
przeprosić	przeproszę / przeprosisz	przeprosił	Przeproś!	pardon
dostawać	dostaję / dostajesz	dostawał		to get /
dostać	dostanę / dostaniesz	dostał		to receive

wierzyć	wierzę / wierzysz	wierzył	Wierz!	to believe
uwierzyć	uwierzę / uwierzysz	uwierzył	Uwierz!	
kochać	kocham / kochasz	kochał	Kochaj!	to love
pokochać	pokocham / pokochasz	pokochał	Pokochaj!	
wracać	wracam / wracasz	wracał	Wracaj!	to return / come back
wrócić	wrócę / wrócisz	wrócił	Wróć!	
znajdować	znajduję / znajdujesz	znajdował	Znajduj!	to find
znaleźć	znajdę / znajdziesz	znalazł	Znajdź!	
stać	stoję / stoisz	stał	Stój!	to stand / to stop
stanąć	stanę / staniesz	stanął	Stań!	
zapominać	zapominam / zapominasz	zapominał	Zapominaj!	to forget
zapomnieć	zapomnę / zapomniesz	zapomniał	Zapomnij!	
zaczynać	zaczynam / zaczynasz	zaczynał	Zaczynaj!	to begin
zacząć	zacznę / zaczniesz	zaczął	Zacznij!	
przyjeżdżać	przyjeżdżam / przyjeżdżasz	przyjeżdżał	Przyjeżdżaj!	to arrive (by transport)
przyjechać	przyjadę / przyjedziesz	przyjechał	Przyjedź!	
przestawać	przestaję / przestajesz	przestawał	Przestawaj!	to stop
przestać	przestanę / przestaniesz	przestał	Przestań!	
pomagać	pomagam / pomagasz	pomagał	Pomagaj!	to help
pomóc	pomogę / pomożesz	pomógł	Pomóż!	
woleć	wolę / wolisz	wolał		to prefer
pytać	pytam / pytasz	pytał	Pytaj!	to ask
zapytać	zapytam / zapytasz	zapytał	Zapytaj!	
zostawiać	zostawiam / zostawiasz	zostawiał	Zostawiaj!	to leave behind
zostawić	zostawię / zostawisz	zostawił	Zostaw!	
umieć	umiem / umiesz	umiał		know how
pisać	piszę / piszesz	pisał	Pisz!	to write
napisać	napiszę / napiszesz	napisał	Napisz!	
szukać	szukam / szukasz	szukał	Szukaj!	to look for
poszukać	poszukam / poszukasz	poszukał	Poszukaj!	
jechać	jadę / jedziesz	jechał	Jedź!	to go / to drive
pojechać	pojadę / pojedziesz	pojechał	Pojedź!	
pozwalać	pozwalam / pozwalasz	pozwalał	Pozwlj!	to allow
pozwolić	pozwolę / pozwolisz	pozwolił	Pozwól!	
mieszkać	mieszkam / mieszkasz	mieszkał	Mieszkaj!	to reside
pracować	pracuję / pracujesz	pracował	Pracuj!	to work
potrafić	potrafię / potrafisz	potrafił		be capable
spać	śpię / śpisz	spał	Śpij!	to sleep
zamykać	zamykam / zamykasz	zamykał	Zamykaj!	to close
zamknąć	zamknę / zamkniesz	zamknął	Zamknij!	
wyglądać	wyglądam / wyglądasz	wyglądał	Wyglądaj!	to look
trzymać	trzymam / trzymasz	trzymał	Trzymaj!	to hold
potrzymać	potrzymam / potrzymasz	potrzymał	Potrzymaj!	
studiować	studiuję / studiujesz	studiował	Studiuj!	to study
grać	gram / grasz	grał	Graj!	to play
zagrać	zagram / zagrasz	zagrał	Zagraj!	
leżeć	leżę / leżysz	leżał	Leż!	to lie down
potrzebować	potrzebuję / potrzebujesz	potrzebował		to need
sprzedawać	sprzedaję / sprzedajesz	sprzedawał	Sprzedawaj!	to sell
sprzedać	sprzedam / sprzedasz	sprzedał	Sprzedaj!	
kupować	kupuję / kupujesz	kupował	Kupuj!	to buy
kupić	kupię / kupisz	kupił	Kup!	
budzić się	budzę się / budzisz się	budził się	Budź!	to wake up
czuć	czuję / czujesz	czuł	Czuj!	to feel / to smell
poczuć	poczuję / poczujesz	poczuł	Poczuj!	

Appendix III: Verb Cards
• Photocopy the following pages, cut out the cards, and fill in the verbs.

Być	Mieć
(ja) jestem (my) jesteśmy	(ja) ___ ___ ___ (my) ___ ___ ___ ___
(ty) jesteś (wy) jesteście	(ty) ___ ___ ___ (wy) ___ ___ ___ ___ ___
(on/a) jest (oni/e) są	(on/a) ___ ___ (oni/e) ___ ___ ___ ___
L form sing. - był / a	L form sing. - ___ ___ ___ ___ / ___
L form plur. -byli / były	L form plur.- ___ ___ ___ ___ ___ / ___ ___
Imprerative: Bądź!	Imperative: Miej!
Rozumieć	**Bać się**
(ja) (my)	(ja) (my)
(ty) (wy)	(ty) (wy)
(on/a) (oni/e)	(on/a) (oni/e)
L form sing. -	L form sing. -
L form plur. -	L form plur. -
Imperative: Zrozum!	Imperative: Bój się!
_____	_____
(ja) (my)	(ja) (my)
(ty) (wy)	(ty) (wy)
(on/a) (oni/e)	(on/a) (oni/e)
L form sing. -	L form sing. -
L form plur. -	L form plur. -
Imperative:	Imperative:
_____	_____
(ja) (my)	(ja) (my)
(ty) (wy)	(ty) (wy)
(on/a) (oni/e)	(on/a) (oni/e)
L form sing. -	L form sing. -
L form plur. -	L form plur. -
Imperative:	Imperative:

Verb Cards

_____	_____
(ja)　　　　(my) (ty)　　　　(wy) (on/a)　　　(oni/e) L form sing. - L form plur. - Imperative:	(ja)　　　　(my) (ty)　　　　(wy) (on/a)　　　(oni/e) L form sing. - L form plur. - Imperative:
_____ (ja)　　　　(my) (ty)　　　　(wy) (on/a)　　　(oni/e) L form sing. - L form plur. - Imperative:	_____ (ja)　　　　(my) (ty)　　　　(wy) (on/a)　　　(oni/e) L form sing. - L form plur. - Imperative:
_____ (ja)　　　　(my) (ty)　　　　(wy) (on/a)　　　(oni/e) L form sing. - L form plur. - Imperative:	_____ (ja)　　　　(my) (ty)　　　　(wy) (on/a)　　　(oni/e) L form sing. - L form plur. - Imperative:
_____ (ja)　　　　(my) (ty)　　　　(wy) (on/a)　　　(oni/e) L form sing. - L form plur. - Imperative:	_____ (ja)　　　　(my) (ty)　　　　(wy) (on/a)　　　(oni/e) L form sing. - L form plur. - Imperative:

Appendix IV: Answers to Exercises

Exercise 1:
Ten: dobry, biały, tani, niski, przystojny, długopis, ołówek, mężczyzna, stół, pies
Ta: mała, wysoka, mądra, czerwona, długa książka, kobieta, nauczycielka, farba, kawa
To: smaczne, stare, drogie, duże dziecko, piwo,
Te: smaczne, stare, drogie, duże okulary, drzwi

Exercise 2: 1: dałbym 2: byłbyś
3: zobaczyłby 4: kochalibyśmy / kochałybyśmy
5: przeczytaliby / przeczytałyby 6: myślałyby
7: kupiłaby

Exercise 3:
1: Gdyby przeczytał gazetę, wiedziałby o tym.
2: Gdyby mieli pieniądze, mogliby to kupić.
3: Gdybyś kochała mnie, mógłbym spać.
4: Gdybym była bogata, mieszkałabym w pałacu.

Exercise 4:
1: Ten ołówek jest nowy.
2: Ta książka jest droga.
3: To piwo jest zimne.
4: Te okulary są stare.
5: To dziecko jest młode.
6: Te drzwi są duże.
7: Ta szklanka jest mała.
8: Ten dom jest zielony.
9: Ta nauczycielka jest mądra.
10: Ten mężczyzna jest wysoki.

Exercise 5:
1: Mam psa.
2: Mamy lampę.
3: Ta pani ma torbę.
4: Andrzej ma portfel.
5: Ten rolnik ma konia.
6: Mają telewizor.

Exercise 6:
1: Dawid i Halina mają białego psa.
2: Michał zna moją siostrę.
3: Ania czyta długą książkę.
4: Zosia czeka na jego brata.
5: Czy ona kupi nową sukienkę?
6: Grzegorz prowadzi niebieski samochód.
7: Wasz dom ma duże okno.

Exercise 7:
1: To jest pies Anny.
2: To jest książka Bolesława Prusa.
3: To jest artykuł Joanny Mizielińskiej.
4: To jest pies Jana.
5: To jest samochód mojego ojca.
6: To jest dom mojej matki.

Exercise 8:
1: On nie pije mocnej kawy.
2: Oni nie lubią tej polskiej piosenki.
3: Agnieszka nie zna profesora Czaplinskiego.
4: Mirek nie studiuje filologii angielskiej.
5: Nie chcemy kupić tego nowego komputera.

Exercise 9:
1: Szukam swojej książi.
2: Lubię słuchać nowoczesnej muzyki.
3: Uczę się języka polskiego.
4: Ja tylko potrzebuję małego słownika.
5: Szukamy dobrego piwa.

Exercise 10:
1: Wieczorem idziemy do mojej babci.
2: Do kogo idziecie?
3: Anna mieszka teraz u ciotki.
4: To jest rower dla mojego brata.
5: Jesteśmy tutaj od poniedziałku.

Exercise 11:
1: Adam jest młodym Amerykaninem.
2: Jenny jest młodą Amerykanki.
3: Kim był Jacques Chirac?
4: Jacques Chirac był prezydentem Francji.
5: Agata jest lekarką.
6: Ireniusz jest lekarz.

Exercise 12.
1: Kot leży pod stołem.
2: Ptak leci nad drzewem.
3: Poczta stoi między sklepem a biblioteką.
4: Przed naszym mieszkaniem jest ładny park.
5: Za budynkiem jest parking.

Exercise 13:
1: Ja zawsze jeżdżę do pracy autobusem.
2: Pojedziemy do Kanady pociągiem.
3: Lecą do Polski samolotem.
4: Wolę pisać długopisem.

Exercise 14:
1: W tej butelce jest wino.
2: Wczoraj byłam na zebraniu z profesorem.
3: Musiał leżeć w łóżku przez dwa dni.
4: Po obiedzie pójdę na spacer.
5: Mieszkam w Krakowie przy pałacu Chuczyńskich.
6: Chcę iść po tym ładnym lesie.
7: Co czytasz w gazecie.
8: O kim mówicie.
9: Dlaczego ten kot leży na moim stole?
10: Będę czekała na ciebie w restauracji.

Exercise 15:
1: Co dałeś mamie?
2: Jeden student dał profesorowi prezent.
3: Czy powiesz ojcu o tym?
4: Czy jest ci za zimno?
5: Ale! Ona bardzo mi się podoba!!
6: Dzięki niej mogę pójść na koncert.
7: Czym przyglądasz się?
8: Pokażemy Janowi nasze zdjęcie.
9: Czy możecie nam pożyczyć te książki?
10: Dzięki waszej pomocy zdałem mój egzamin.

Exercise 16:
1: Ile kosztują te książki.
2: Te dwa domy należą do Jana.
3: Są cztery duże miasta w Polsce.
4: Te dwie siostry zawsze kłócą się.
5: Dokąd jadą te dwa pociągi?

Exercise 17:
1: Tu pracują bardzo dobrzy profesorowie.
2: Skąd są ci Polacy?
3: Znani aktorzy mieszkają tam.
4: Czy wasi kuzynowie mają samochody?
5: Jacy są twoi nauczyciele?

Exercise 18:
1: Jan ma trzy duże mieszkania.
2: Proszę cztery małe piwa.
3: Czy czytałaś te ciekawe ksążki?
4: Ile psów masz?
5: Nie kupił tych nowych butów.
6: Czy ona zna twoich trzech bratów?
7: Tych sześciu aktorów jest bardzo znanych.
8: Których dziewczyn nie ma na zajęciu dzisiaj?
9: To jest dom naszych rodziców.
10: Ile książek czytaliście ostatniego roku?

Exercise 19:
1: Poszedłem do baru z moimi studentami.
2: Jechali do Polski dwoma samolotami i trzema pociągami.
3: "Macbeth" i "Romeo i Julia" są dramatami Szekspira.
4: Wiewórki stoją pod drzewami.
5: Jakimi pisarzami interesujesz się?

Exercise 20:
1: Buty leżą przy drzwiach.
2: W tych miastach mieszkają dużo Polaków.
3: Czy myślisz o swoich egzaminach?
4: Jej koty śpią na je czerwoncy kanapach.
5: Po tych ulicach chodzi dużo psów

•**NOTES**

•NOTES

•NOTES

www.ingramcontent.com/pod-product-compliance
Lightning Source LLC
Chambersburg PA
CBHW051709040426
42446CB00008B/795